Holding My E
(Na-Fa-Sam)

The Story of an Afghan American Woman

By:
Sami N.

Before getting started, I wanted to say that all the people mentioned in my story have been changed to pseudonym names for privacy and the protection of their identities.

Table of Contents

Introduction

For the past three years, I hesitated to write about my life. Every day, I found a reason to silence my voice, to keep my story hidden. Yet, one evening, as I sat in a dimly lit hookah lounge, I asked myself, "Why not? Why shouldn't I share my journey, the reality of being an Afghan American woman in this country?" Each of us carries a story, and mine has shaped the woman I am today: resilient, independent, and constantly searching for reasons to keep going.

I write this with the hope that my experiences might reach those who feel lost and hopeless to show that even in the darkest moments, you can endure. Life has thrown its share of trials my way, yet here I stand, unbroken. But I want to be honest, waking up every day is still a battle, a struggle to find the will to continue.

I choose to remain anonymous not out of fear but because I'm not ready for my family to learn my truth—the secrets I've harbored for 29 years. My childhood was filled with a deep hatred for life, so much so that I believed the only escape from my suffering was death. I attempted to end my life more than four times: overdosing on painkillers, contemplating driving off a cliff, and even cutting my wrists in a bathtub. Each time, just as I teetered on the edge of success, something pulled me back. That something was my mother.

She never knew what I was trying to do, but her presence would fill my thoughts. Sometimes, I'd hear her footsteps in the middle of the night, the sound reminding me of her strength. My mother has been a warrior her entire life, battling multiple sclerosis for the past 12 years. At one point,

She was paralyzed for a year and spent a month in a coma. When she woke up, she had temporarily lost her memory. Now, at the age of 62, she walks and works every day despite the occasional seizures. She never lets these challenges defeat her. I realized that if I ended my life, it would be the most selfish act imaginable; it would destroy her. I am her world, and without me, she wouldn't survive. I want my mother to live as long as she can, and I know that leaving this earth by suicide would break not just her but many others who care for me.

Chapter: 1
The Beginning

Let me start by sharing my story so you can understand the journey that shaped me. My parents are both immigrants from Kabul, Afghanistan, a fact that should immediately signal the complexity of my upbringing. Life was never easy, not for them and certainly not for me, their only child. In our Afghan household, the weight of expectations and the responsibility I bore were immense. Being an only child, I was the center of their hopes but also the target of their frustrations and fears. The cultural standards I had to live up to were rigorous, leaving little room for error or individuality.

Love was a foreign concept to me; instead, I was shown what my parents considered "tough love." Independence was drilled into me from an early age; I was taught to never ask for help, no matter how much I struggled. My father was the enforcer of these ideals, a man who never learned how to express affection. Strict to the point of harshness, he believed that breaking me down would build me up stronger. But he was wrong.

The verbal abuse was relentless, words meant to cut, to instill discipline, but all they did was wound my already fragile spirit. I was sensitive, yearning for validation and acceptance, always seeking approval from those around me. I believed that if people didn't like me, it was because I wasn't good enough, that there was something inherently wrong with me. But the truth was, the problem wasn't with me; it was with the world I was forced to navigate.

Physical abuse was also a common occurrence in our home, and it wasn't just a light slap on the wrist. My father's discipline often turned brutal, my head bashed against walls, my body bruised and battered. I'd be locked in my room for days, deprived of food and water, left to suffer in silence. My father never listened to me, never gave me a chance to explain. He preferred to believe the lies others told him, even when those lies came from family.

My father believed that physical punishment was the most effective way to teach me lessons and prevent me from making mistakes. But this wasn't just a spank on the butt, his punishments were merciless and relentless. It became second nature for him to use his fists to communicate his disappointment, anger, or fear. The violence escalated to the where I would be battered and bruised or forbidden to eat or drink anything. The physical pain was excruciating, but it was the emotional and psychological torment that cut deeper.

My father never gave me the benefit of the doubt, especially when it came to my behavior. One of the most hurtful betrayals came from my own cousin, a person bound to me by blood. Out of jealousy or spite, she spread vicious rumors that I was sleeping with men and had multiple boyfriends when I was only 12 years old. I was still a child, naive and innocent, barely aware of what a crush was, let alone anything more. Her lies poisoned the already fragile relationship I had with my father, further severing any chance of understanding between us, shattered completely. The damage she caused was irreparable.

The fallout was immediate and harsh. My father's paranoia took over, and I was placed under constant surveillance. Every morning, I was watched as I walked to school, my interactions scrutinized and monitored. Boys were forbidden from even looking in my direction, and any who dared to do so would face my father's wrath. My life became a tightly controlled prison, where every move I made was dictated by his fears and suspicions.

These experiences shaped my early life, forcing me to grow up under the shadow of fear and mistrust. The wounds inflicted by my father's harshness and my cousin's deception left scars that I carry with me to this day. But these scars also tell the story of my survival, of the battles I fought and continue to fight.

In the midst of this oppressive environment, I faced yet another challenge during middle school. I received two bad grades on my report card, C's, which I knew would trigger a furious response from my parents, especially my father. Terrified of the consequences, I took a pencil and, with trembling hands, altered the grades to B's. Somehow, despite my fear, I managed to make the changes look legitimate. When I showed the report card to my parents, they were pleased, their smiles masking the storm that was about to come.

The relief I felt was short-lived. I hadn't realized that the school also mailed a copy of the report card home. One morning, I woke up to the sound of my father downstairs, opening the mail. My heart raced as I walked down the stairs, forcing a casual "Good morning," but all I received in return was an icy silence. I glanced at the table and saw the report card, the one with my actual grades. My blood ran cold. I knew I was in deep trouble. My father didn't say a word, but his silence was more terrifying than any shouting could have been.

Later that day, during 3rd period, I was called to the counselor's office. My stomach churned with anxiety as I walked down the hall, and when I saw my father's car parked outside, my fear intensified. In the office, we sat with the counselor, and I was asked why I had changed my grades. Through tears, I explained that I was terrified of my parents' reaction. The counselor warned me that if something like this happened again, I would face suspension. I could see the rage boiling just beneath my father's calm exterior, and I knew the real punishment was still waiting for me at home.

The ride home was silent, filled with tension so thick it was suffocating. As soon as we entered the house, my father exploded. He beat me savagely, venting all his anger and disappointment on my small frame. He didn't stop there—he stormed into my room, destroying everything in sight. My belongings, my TV, everything was left shattered in his wake. In his fury, he shouted at my mother to give me up for adoption, declaring that he didn't want a daughter like me.

Chapter: 2
Family Gatherings and Betrayal

For the next four days, each one slowly blending into the next, I was locked in my room without food or water, my only company, the empty walls that seemed to close in on me, with loneliness suffocating me. My mother, trapped in her own cycle of fear and worry, would sneak food into my room when my father was out, but I couldn't bring myself to eat. The food would sit there, untouched, as I sat in the darkness, feeling utterly miserable and alone. I slept on the cold, hard floor, feeling more like a convict than a daughter. The despair I felt was overwhelming, and all I could think about was escaping the nightmare that had become my life. But since I was just a child, I didn't know how or even how to ask for help.

This was my reality, a life ruled by fear, violence, and the oppressive expectations of a father who couldn't see beyond his own pain and anger. And the betrayal by my cousin only deepened my isolation, leaving me trapped in a world where the people who should have protected me were the ones who hurt me the most.

Even when the punishment was over, I didn't want to leave my room. The very thought of facing my parents, especially my father, filled me with dread. I understood that what I did was wrong, but the way my father handled the situation felt wildly disproportionate. It wasn't just about the punishment; it was about the overwhelming sense of fear and helplessness that came with it.

After four long days, we had to go to my grandparents' house for a traditional gathering. My grandfather had passed away about three weeks prior, and in our culture, we observe 40 days of prayer to honor the deceased. I thought that maybe, after everything I had been through, things would finally start to calm down. But instead, they took a turn for the worse.

At the gathering, my older cousin, who had already caused so much turmoil in my life, decided to stir up more trouble. She told my parents that a boy at my middle school had a crush on me and that they needed to be more vigilant about who I was spending time with. Given my father's already heightened paranoia and suspicion, it didn't take much for him to believe her. Once again, I found myself under intense scrutiny.

My phone was taken away, and I was treated like a convicted felon in my own home. My father decided to go through my messages, looking for any signs of impropriety. When he found a text from a boy asking for help on a class project, he flew into a rage. I tried to explain that the boy was just my class partner, that there was nothing inappropriate about our interaction, but my father wouldn't listen. His mind was made up. He believed every word my cousin had said, and in his eyes, I was guilty of being something I was not, a middle school "ho," as he so cruelly put it. In his anger, he ordered me to pack my things and leave the house. I was in shock, my hands shaking as I grabbed a few belongings and my phone when he wasn't looking. I stumbled out of the house, my heart racing, and called my mom, sobbing uncontrollably. I told her that dad had kicked me out, that I didn't know what to do or where to go. My father, hearing my cries, became frantic, worried that the neighbors would hear, and started asking questions. He dragged me back inside, his grip tight and unyielding, and told me to go to my room and not come out.

As I climbed the stairs, the overwhelming stress and anxiety finally took their toll. My vision blurred, and I felt my body go numb. I collapsed on the floor, my body convulsing in a full-blown seizure. I had never had a seizure before, and the experience was terrifying. My father, hearing the commotion, initially thought I was up to something, but when he found me on the floor, his panic set in. He tried to give me CPR, but nothing was working. Desperate, he called the paramedics.

When the paramedics arrived, my father's sister was there, urging me not to say anything about what was really happening at home. But deep down, I wanted to tell them everything. I wanted someone to know that I was being beaten, that I was living in constant fear, that this was not just a medical emergency but a cry for help. The paramedics noticed that every time I was questioned, my heart rate would spike, and they decided to take me to the hospital.

I ended up being hospitalized for three months. During that time, every time my father visited, I would have a seizure. The doctors couldn't control or stabilize my condition, and I was given heavy medication to keep me sedated to prevent the seizures from happening. But the nightmares continued. I would wake up in a panic, screaming and thrashing, convinced that my father was there, hurting me again. The nurses would try to calm me down, but nothing seemed to work. They had to keep increasing the medication just to keep me from spiraling into another episode.

I stayed silent throughout my time in the hospital. I didn't tell anyone what was happening at home. I didn't want to talk, didn't want to see anyone. I withdrew into myself, becoming mute and unresponsive, a shell of who I had been. The medication kept me in a near-constant state of sleep, but even in my dreams, I couldn't escape the trauma.

As the months went by and I started to feel a little better, my father tried to be nicer. He visited less often, and when he did, he seemed more subdued, more careful in his words and actions.

One day, he even told me he was sorry that things had come to this, that he hadn't meant for it to go this far. I believed him, or at least I wanted to. I knew that he wanted me to learn a lesson, but I also knew that he didn't want me to be hospitalized, that he hadn't intended to almost kill me. But despite his apologies, the damage was done. The trust between us, if there had ever been any, was completely shattered. I knew that things would never be the same, that I could never feel safe in my own home again. The hospital had become my refuge, a place where, despite the constant fear and the heavy medication, I was at least out of my father's reach.

When I was 12 years old, I thought I had started my period. I was a bit nervous but also curious about this new chapter of my life. I quickly ran to my mom and told her I was bleeding. She smiled softly and reassured me that it was just my period, a normal part of growing up. But as the days passed, the bleeding didn't stop. Instead of fading away as I expected, it continued, and soon, I was overwhelmed by severe stomach pains and relentless vomiting. My young mind couldn't comprehend what was happening to my body, and fear began to creep in.

Concerned, my parents took me to the doctor. The visit was a blur of sterile smells and worried faces. After a series of examinations, the doctor delivered news that shook us all: this wasn't a period at all, I was internally bleeding from my stomach and needed to be taken to the hospital immediately. The urgency in the doctor's voice turned my fear into panic.

When I arrived at the hospital, the reality of the situation began to sink in. The cold, impersonal environment made me feel small and vulnerable. I was rushed through a series of tests, each more invasive and uncomfortable than the last. The doctors discovered that I had 12 ulcers, and a couple of them had ruptured, causing internal bleeding. The news hit me like a ton of bricks, I needed emergency surgery to remove the ulcers, and I was terrified. I had never had surgery before and didn't know what to expect. The thought of being cut open, of the pain and the unknown, filled me with dread.

The surgery lasted about eight hours, an eternity for someone so young and scared. When I woke up, I was groggy and in pain but relieved that it was over. I was hospitalized for about a week, gradually moving from a liquid diet to solid food. The process was slow and painful, but I was excited to go home, especially because we had planned a trip to Paris to see my grandfather the following week. It was a trip I had been looking forward to for months.

But my excitement was short-lived. As soon as I got home, I found that I couldn't keep any food or water down. Every time I tried to eat or drink, I would vomit it all backup. My parents, alarmed and worried, rushed me back to urgent care. The doctors were puzzled, they couldn't figure out what was going wrong. They put me on a feeding tube and ran test after test, trying to diagnose the problem. After two agonizing weeks of uncertainty, they finally discovered the cause: I had a rare disease called achalasia, a condition where the esophagus doesn't function properly, making it difficult to swallow.

Chapter: 3
Weight of Survival

I was the second person in the entire United States to be diagnosed with this disease at the time, and my doctors were at a loss. They had never dealt with a case like mine and didn't know how to treat it. They brought in a specialist from a different hospital, a renowned GI doctor with more knowledge and experience. When the specialist reviewed my case, he said I needed another surgery. I felt completely overwhelmed, the weight of my situation pressing down on me.

I didn't want another surgery, and I definitely didn't want to stay in the hospital any longer. Of course, I had no choice or vote in the matter. The second surgery was even longer than the first, it was about 10 hours. The doctors took my esophagus and tied it to my stomach to reduce the pressure, hoping this would alleviate the problem. The recovery was grueling. I was in the hospital for four more days, waiting until I could finally drink liquids without vomiting. When I was finally able to drink, the doctors were cautiously optimistic and sent me home.

That night, my mom made me homemade soup with soft noodles and vegetables. I was so excited to finally eat something after weeks of being on a feeding tube. But as soon as I took a bite, I felt the familiar, nauseating sensation in my stomach. I barely made it to the bathroom before I vomited everything back up. I felt utterly defeated. Once again, my parents rushed me back to the hospital.

The doctors were baffled. They didn't understand why the surgery had failed. They ordered more tests, and when the results came back, it showed that the way my esophagus had been tied was too tight, restricting the passage of food. I needed another surgery, my third in just a few short weeks. This time, I couldn't hold back the tears. I cried uncontrollably, not understanding why this was happening to me, why my body was betraying me like this.

Instead of another major surgery, the doctors suggested a less invasive procedure where they would insert a temporary balloon inside me to help me eat. They assured me that this would give my body some time to heal. My parents agreed, and I prepared for the procedure. Before they could proceed, however, they needed to conduct a test where they would insert a tube through my nose and down my throat to take pictures. The test required me to be fully awake, and the pain was indescribable. I screamed and cried, begging my mom to take me home, to let me die, because I couldn't endure the pain any longer. The nurses had to hold me down as I kicked and thrashed, desperately trying to escape the agony. The test lasted over an hour, each minute feeling like an eternity. By the end of it, I was completely drained, both physically and emotionally. I felt like I was being punished for something I didn't even understand.

I sank into a deep depression. The constant pain, the surgeries, the fear, it all became too much to bear. I didn't want to live like this anymore. The thought of facing another procedure, another round of pain and uncertainty, was unbearable. But I had no choice. I counted the upcoming procedure as my fourth surgery, even though it wasn't technically surgery. The doctors reassured me that everything went well and that if I could eat the next day, I could go home.

But my hopes were dashed once again when the balloon didn't even last a day before rupturing inside me. I was taken in for my fifth surgery. By this point, I was beyond exhausted. I remember lying on the operating table, looking up at the doctors and telling them to just let me die, that I was tired and didn't want to do this anymore. I was only 12 years old, but I felt like I had lived through a lifetime of pain and suffering.

The fifth surgery was the longest one yet, lasting over 24 hours. I don't remember much from that time. I kept slipping in and out of consciousness, my mind foggy from the pain and the medication. Every time I woke up, I saw my mom by my bedside, talking quietly to my family members who had come to visit. I could feel the love and concern around me, but I felt disconnected from it all. I was too lost in my own world of pain.

The nurses had to spray something in my throat every four hours to keep me sedated and to prevent me from feeling the pain. I would drift in and out of sleep, not knowing what was real and what was a dream. At one point, I woke up and saw my mom talking to my uncle. I reached out and grabbed her hand, holding on to the one constant in my life that gave me comfort. Before long, I slipped back into unconsciousness.

When I woke up again, I was alone in my room. The silence was deafening, and I started to shake uncontrollably. I tried to speak, to call out for someone, but nothing came out. A nurse walking by saw me shaking and came to check on me. She sat on my bed and asked what I needed. I wrote down on a piece of paper that I couldn't breathe. She looked me straight in the eyes and told me that I was breathing just fine, that my oxygen levels were normal. But I knew something was wrong. I tried to keep her from leaving, grabbing my throat as if to show her that I was struggling to get air. That's when I started coding.

The next thing I remember was waking up in the ICU, surrounded by machines and monitors. I looked around and saw my family standing outside my room, looking in through a window. They weren't allowed in the room, and the sight of them standing there, helpless and worried, broke my heart. A nurse came in and explained what had happened: I had an allergic reaction to the spray they had been giving me every four hours, and it had caused my heart to stop for about a minute.

The thought of how close I had come to dying was terrifying. I spent the next three nights and four days in the ICU, alone and scared. No family was allowed in, and I felt like I was living in a nightmare. I kept thinking about how I wanted to say goodbye to my parents, to tell them how much I loved them, just in case I didn't make it. I wanted to tell my dad that I was sorry I wasn't the daughter he wanted, that no matter what, I still loved him.

When I was finally released from the ICU and moved back into a regular room, visitation was allowed again. My mom was the first to come in, and I immediately asked her to lay next to me and just hold me. She started crying, telling me everything was going to be okay. Somehow, I could tell something off. I hadn't seen my dad, and I wondered where he was. My mom explained that I had been in the hospital for about four months, and he needed to go to work to pay for everything.

As the days passed, I overheard my mom talking on the phone, her voice low but animated, as if she was planning something. It sounded like she was organizing a party or some kind of gathering, and a wave of anger surged through me. I couldn't believe what I was hearing. How could she even think of celebrating anything when I was lying there, barely holding on? The idea of her planning a party while I felt like I was on my deathbed made me furious.

I looked at my mom, my emotions boiling over. "How can you plan a party when I'm lying here like this?" I snapped at her, my voice trembling with a mix of anger and despair. I couldn't understand how she could be thinking about anything other than my situation. I felt betrayed like my suffering wasn't even significant enough to pause her life.

She turned to me, her face pale and her eyes full of sadness. She didn't know how to tell me what was really happening, and for a moment, there was just silence between us. When she finally spoke, her voice was soft and hesitant. "I wasn't planning a party," she said. "Four days ago, while you were in the ICU, your grandfather, the one you were supposed to see in Paris, passed away."

Her words hit me like a physical blow. The anger I felt was instantly replaced by a feeling of deep, overwhelming sorrow. I broke down, tears streaming down my face as the weight of her words sank in. I felt an intense sense of guilt wash over me, a guilt that didn't make sense but was all-consuming nonetheless. My mind kept telling me that it wasn't my fault that I got sick. Yet, in some twisted way, I felt solely responsible for all of it. Even though I knew rationally that I had no control over my illness or the timing of everything that had happened, I still felt like my illness had stolen my father's precious chance to say goodbye to his own father, a moment that he would never get back. This loss was overwhelming, and the guilt that I couldn't shake, that I had somehow contributed to it, sat there in my heart, constantly gnawing at me.

The realization that my grandfather was gone and that I would never see him again was devastating. I had been looking forward to our trip to Paris, to seeing him and spending time with him. And now, all of that is gone, just like that. The opportunity to say goodbye, to be there for my dad in his time of grief, had slipped away while I was lying in a hospital bed, fighting for my own life.

As I cried, my mom came over and held me, her own tears mingling with mine. She tried to comfort me, telling me that it wasn't my fault, that no one could have predicted any of this. Unfortunately, her words, though kind and meant to be soothing, did little to soothe the ache in my heart. I was consumed by the grief of losing my grandfather and the guilt of what my illness had cost my family.

Chapter: 4
Fragile Steps to Healing

It was a moment that marked me, one that added yet another layer of pain to an already overwhelming situation. And as I lay there, holding onto my mom, I couldn't help but think about how fragile and unpredictable life could be, how quickly everything could change. It was a harsh reminder that some losses were permanent and that the impact of those losses could ripple through our lives in ways we couldn't even begin to comprehend.

After hearing the news about my grandfather, I felt trapped in the sterile confines of the hospital, surrounded by machines and monitors, longing for a connection to the outside world. I asked my mom to take me outside to feel the fresh air on my face and see something beyond the hospital walls. She gently agreed, placing me in a wheelchair and wrapping me in blankets to protect me from the chill. It was my first time in four months seeing the world beyond my hospital room, and the moment was both exhilarating and heartbreaking.

As we reached the terrace of the hospital, the cool breeze brushed against my skin, and I took a deep breath, savoring the simple pleasure of fresh air. Then I saw him, my dad, standing off to the side, tears streaming down his face. It was a sight I had rarely witnessed: my father, usually so strong and stoic, was broken by grief. The image of him crying was like a punch to the gut, and I felt the weight of everything I had been carrying intensify.

I wheeled myself over to him and grabbed his hand, the touch connecting us in a way words couldn't. "I'm so sorry," I whispered, my voice trembling with emotion. "I'm so sorry you couldn't say goodbye to your dad. It's my fault." My dad didn't say anything; he just squeezed my hand, his grip firm yet tender. The silence between us was heavy with unspoken feelings, but in that moment, it was enough. He didn't need to say anything; his presence, his tears, spoke volumes. That night, as my parents waited for me to fall asleep so they could grab something to eat, I felt an overwhelming exhaustion wash over me. The emotional weight of everything, the surgeries, the illness, the loss of my grandfather, had drained me completely. I drifted off into what I thought would be a peaceful sleep.

Suddenly, in the middle of the night, everything changed. I started coding again, my body betraying me once more. I vaguely remember hearing my dad's voice, filled with panic, screaming my name. It was a desperate, heart-wrenching sound unlike anything I had ever heard from him before. When I woke up later, I had no idea what had happened. The room was filled with doctors and nurses, their faces etched with concern. They couldn't understand what was going on, and neither could I.

The doctors speculated that my body was reacting to the emotional stress, the depression that had settled over me after hearing about my grandfather's passing. They decided to put me on antidepressants to help relax me, hoping to stabilize my condition. The days that followed were a blur of emptiness and isolation. I would wake up to an empty room, my parents absent as they prepared for the funeral. The loneliness was suffocating. I wanted to be at my grandfather's ceremony, to honor him, to say goodbye in my own way, even though I hadn't been able to do so in person. Instead, I was trapped in a room with no windows, staring at a blank wall, feeling more alone than ever.

I cried for days, the sorrow consuming me. The silence of the hospital, the absence of my parents, and the knowledge that life was moving on without me made the days stretch endlessly. I felt disconnected from the world, separated from everything that had once mattered to me. It was as if time had stopped for me while the rest of the world kept spinning.

Two long weeks passed before I was finally discharged. The doctors monitored my progress closely, and I slowly began to regain the ability to eat and drink. After four excruciatingly long months, I was finally able to go home. The thought of returning to the familiarity of my house, of starting to rebuild my life, was both exciting and daunting. I was no longer the same person who had entered the hospital months ago; I had been through too much, and those experiences had altered me.

As I stepped back into my home, I felt a mixture of relief and trepidation, but finally being home. I was ready to start getting back to being a kid, but I knew that the journey ahead wouldn't be easy. I had to learn how to live again, how to move past the pain and loss, and how to find joy in the little things once more. Being home after being in the hospital for so long was the best feeling I'd had in months. The familiar sights and smells of my house were a comfort, even though I wasn't able to fully walk yet and still needed all the help I could get. My body was weak, and every movement reminded me of the long road to recovery that lay ahead. But just being home, surrounded by the things and people I loved, made me feel like I was finally on the mend.

As the weeks passed, I slowly began to regain some of my strength. But I was far from the active, carefree kid I had been before. I had to be careful with everything I did, every step, every movement—because my body was still fragile. I couldn't carry anything heavier than three pounds, which meant I couldn't wear a regular backpack like the other kids. Instead, I was forced to use a roller backpack.

The new school semester was starting, and I was filled with a mix of excitement and dread. I wanted to go back to school to be around other kids again, but the thought of returning with a roller backpack filled me with anxiety. In middle school, a roller backpack was practically a social death sentence. I knew that it would make me stand out in all the wrong ways, but I didn't have a choice.

On the first day of school, I rolled my backpack into the building, trying to ignore the stares and whispers. As I walked from class to class, the other kids didn't hold back. They made fun of me, laughing and calling me names, and some even kicked my backpack as I passed by. I tried to brush it off, to pretend it didn't bother me, but inside, I felt humiliated. I was already dealing with so much, my body still weak, my emotions raw from everything I had been through, and now I had to face this on top of it.

That day, when I got home, I broke down. I told my parents everything about how the kids had teased me and how I couldn't bear to go back. The thought of facing another day at school, of being the target of ridicule, was too much. I begged them to let me stay home and find another way for me to keep up with my studies. My parents, seeing how much I was struggling, agreed to homeschool me for the rest of the year.

Being homeschooled was both a relief and a new kind of challenge. On one hand, I didn't have to deal with the teasing and bullying at school, but on the other hand, I became very isolated. I spent most of my days alone, with only my books and my thoughts for company. The friends I once had drifted away, and I didn't make any new ones. I became increasingly antisocial, withdrawing into myself more and more with each passing day. The world outside my home became something distant and unfamiliar, something I didn't really know how to be a part of anymore.

You could say my life became like being incarcerated, albeit one with better food and the comfort of home, but the isolation weighed heavily on me. I missed the simple interactions with others, the laughter, and even the arguments that came with being around people my own age.

My days were filled with schoolwork, but the lack of social interaction made me feel like I was losing touch with the outside world. The house that had once been my refuge now felt like a cage, and I longed for the freedom to just be a kid again.

The following year, whether I liked it or not, I had to return to school on the school premises. It was a daunting prospect, I wasn't ready to face the world again, but staying isolated at home was no longer an option. My body had healed enough to allow me to attend classes, but the emotional scars were still fresh, and the idea of being back in the school environment filled me with anxiety.

To help ease the transition, the school assigned me a TA, an older gentleman named Mr. Art. He had four daughters of his own, and his gentle, fatherly demeanor made me feel at ease. From the moment we met, I could tell that he genuinely cared about my well-being. He became like my own personal assistant, taking care of everything I needed. He carried my books, helped me navigate the hallways, and made sure that no harm came to me. Even a year after my

surgeries, my stitches were still healing, and I had to be extremely careful to avoid any kind of infection. Mr. Art was there to make sure I was safe. Despite my initial apprehensions, Mr. Art made returning to school bearable. He was kind and attentive, always ready with a smile or a comforting word. He was the kind of person who made you feel like everything was going to be okay, even when it felt like the world was crumbling around you. His presence became a source of comfort in an environment that still felt foreign and frightening.

Chapter: 5
When Silence Breaks

One day, after school, we sat together on the playground, waiting for my parents to pick me up. The sun was setting, casting long shadows across the ground, and the air was filled with the sounds of kids laughing and playing in the distance. But inside, I felt a storm brewing. I had been carrying so much weight on my shoulders, so many secrets and fears, and it all felt like it was too much to bear. I took a deep sigh, and before I knew it, tears started rolling down my face.

Mr. Art noticed immediately. He asked me what was wrong, his voice gentle and full of concern. At first, I didn't want to say anything. I had become so used to keeping everything bottled up inside, afraid of what might happen if I let it all out. But Mr. Art assured me that I could trust him, that he would always keep me safe. There was something in his voice, a sincerity that made me feel like maybe, just maybe, it was okay to open up.

So, I began to tell him everything. I told him about the surgeries, the pain, the isolation. I told him about my father's anger, about the fear that hung over our household like a dark cloud. I told him things I had never told anyone before, things I had been too scared or ashamed to admit. Mind you, I was barely 13 years old at the time, but I had already experienced more than most people could imagine. Mr. Art listened intently, his expression a mix of sadness and concern. When I finished, he promised me that our conversation would stay completely between us. I believed him. I trusted him.

Two days later, I had just gotten home from school with my parents when there was a knock on the door. My heart skipped a beat, a sense of dread washing over me as my mom went to answer it. Standing on the other side were representatives from Child Services. They informed my parents that there had been a report of child abuse, and I could see the shock and confusion on my parents' faces. They couldn't understand what was happening.

The next moments were a blur. The Child Services workers tried to take me away from my parents, and my mom begged them not to take me. It was at that moment, as I watched the chaos unfold around me that I realized what had happened. Mr. Art had reported my parents.

He had broken his promise to keep our conversation between us. Fear and guilt twisted in my stomach. I was too afraid to tell my parents that I knew what was happening, too scared of what they might do or say.

I was taken to a foster home, placed with a bunch of other kids who had also been removed from their families. The experience was terrifying. The foster home was unfamiliar and cold, and I was surrounded by strangers. I was scared out of my mind, worried that I would never see my parents again. Despite everything that had happened at home, I didn't want to be in the foster care system. I wanted to go back to my parents. Good or bad, they were still my family, and I wanted to be with them rather than in a strange, unfamiliar place.

I spent a day in the foster home, a day that felt like it stretched on forever before I was finally able to go back home. My dad had figured out what was going on. He went to my school and got Mr. Art fired. He told the school that the allegations were all false and that I was living in a loving, safe home. Child Services eventually allowed me to return home, but they kept my family under investigation for a while longer.

When I got back, the atmosphere in the house was tense. My parents didn't talk to me for a month, but during this time, no one beat me, no one locked me in a room, nothing. It was as if everyone was walking on eggshells, trying to pretend that everything was normal, even though it clearly wasn't. The silence was suffocating, but it was better than the alternative.

After the investigation was over and my parents were cleared, life slowly began to return to its uneasy normalcy. My parents eventually sat me down and asked why I had reported them. I didn't know how to explain that I hadn't meant for it to happen, that I had just wanted to confide in someone, that I was scared and overwhelmed and didn't know what else to do. I didn't know how to tell them that I wanted to leave the family because I felt like I was suffocating under the weight of our secrets and the pain of our reality. I couldn't tell them that my father's actions were the reason I had been hospitalized so many times. So, instead, I stayed quiet. I said I didn't know, that I was sorry and that it would never happen again.

My mother was weak, and her weakness manifested in ways that left me exposed and vulnerable to the worst aspects of my father's rage. She never protected me, never stood between us when he would lash out. Instead, she stayed silent, allowing the abuse to unfold as if it were an inevitable part of life. It was as though she had accepted it, internalized the belief that this was her lot, and by extension, mine too. Her silence wasn't just a void—it was an endorsement of the violence that shaped my childhood.

One memory in particular stands out, a moment that encapsulates the helplessness I felt. I was in middle school, just starting to navigate the confusing and often hostile world of adolescence.

There was a boy in my computer class who would make inappropriate comments and gestures towards me. At the time, I didn't fully understand what was happening—I just knew that it made me uncomfortable, that it was wrong. Summoning all the courage I had, I reported his behavior to the principal, believing that the adults in my life would protect me.

But instead of receiving help, my situation became even more dangerous. The principal, rather than addressing the issue directly, contacted my aunt—my father's sister. I don't know what I expected, but I certainly didn't anticipate what happened next. My aunt, fully aware of how

volatile and abusive my father could be, chose to go to him with the information instead of helping me. She knew what would happen, knew the kind of man her brother was, and yet she made a choice that would lead to one of the most terrifying nights of my life.

That night is seared into my memory. My father was waiting for me when I got home, his face a mask of fury. Without a word, he grabbed me by the hair and dragged me outside to the car. The cold night air stung my skin, but it was nothing compared to the fear that gripped me. He pulled me roughly towards the car, and before I could react, he bashed my head against the car window. The pain was immediate and blinding, but it didn't stop there. He turned on me with a rage I had never seen before, punching me so hard in the arm that I felt something crack. The bruises that formed were deep and dark, lasting for weeks, a constant reminder of that night.

After the assault, I didn't know where to turn. In my desperation, I went to my mother's family, hoping that they might offer some kind of refuge and some help. I told them everything, how much my parents drank, how erratic and dangerous my father could be. I begged them to intervene, to help me escape the hell that my home had become. But their response was a bitter disappointment to me. They told me that I had to deal with it because these were my parents, and no matter how bad things got, leaving the household would bring shame to the family.

Their words felt like a death sentence. I was trapped, bound by cultural expectations and the fear of dishonoring my family's name. I felt so hopeless and scared, completely alone in my suffering. The idea of going to the police crossed my mind, but I was too terrified.

I didn't want to cause a scandal, didn't want to bring shame upon my family. The fear of what might happen if I spoke out kept me silent. The shame, the fear, and the cultural pressures created a cage that I couldn't escape.

In my desperation, I turned to my mother, the one person who should have been my protector. I asked her, in a voice trembling with pain and confusion, why she never helped me. Why didn't she stand up to him? Why didn't she shield me from his wrath? Her answer was as heartbreaking as it was revealing. She told me she was scared and that she knew how crazy my father was. She admitted that she could never leave him and take me with her without it turning into a fight, a fight she believed she couldn't win. She said she didn't want to put me through that as if the alternative, staying in a home filled with violence and fear—was any better.

Hearing her say that, I felt a sick, twisted sense of understanding. In some parts of my mind, I grasped that she was also a victim, that she too was trapped in this cycle of abuse and fear. But that understanding did nothing to ease my pain. What she didn't realize, what she perhaps never would realize, was that in her inaction, in her silence, she had ruined my life. I was just 12 years old, and no one was there to help me. No one stood up for me. And that knowledge, that sense of abandonment, became a burden I would carry for years to come.

Chapter: 6
Bound by Fear, Broken by Violence

When I was 15, my father left for Afghanistan, and with him went the last semblance of normalcy in my life. His departure meant that I had to step into roles that no teenager should have to fill. I became the caretaker for my sick mother, the one responsible for managing the household finances, and somehow, I still had to keep up with my schoolwork. It was a heavy burden for anyone, let alone a teenager, but I had no choice. My life revolved around bills, medication schedules, and making sure the house didn't fall apart. The idea of a social life was a luxury I couldn't afford.

I didn't have any friends, but I convinced myself that was okay. I didn't have the time or energy to invest in friendships. My days were consumed by responsibilities, and any free time I had was spent trying to keep my head above water. I didn't know what it was like to be a normal teenager, to laugh with friends, or go to the mall. My life was defined by duty and obligation, and I had resigned myself to that reality.

Then something unexpected happened. A new girl transferred to my school, and for some reason, we clicked immediately. She was warm, friendly, and seemed genuinely interested in getting to know me. It was the first real connection I had made in a long time, and it felt like a breath of fresh air in a life that had become stifling. We quickly became best friends, and the fact that she lived just across the street from me made it even better. Walking to and from school with her became the highlight of my day. For those few moments, I could forget about the pressures at home and just be a normal teenager, laughing and talking about silly things.

One day, as we were walking home, she casually mentioned that her older brother had seen me and thought I was very beautiful. She said he wanted to meet me, and in my naive, attention-starved state,

I agreed without a second thought. I was 15, and the idea that someone found me beautiful was exhilarating. I had spent so much time feeling invisible, burdened by responsibilities that no one my age should have, that the thought of being seen, of being desired, was intoxicating.

When I finally met him, let's call him Bill, I was instantly captivated. He was everything my 15-year-old self thought a boy should be: handsome, charming, and attentive. He said all the right things, making me feel special in a way I hadn't felt in a long time, if ever. I was drawn to him, not just because of his looks, but because of the way he made me feel important, valued, and most of all, noticed. I fell for him almost immediately, completely unaware of the dark path I was about to walk down.

In the beginning, everything seemed perfect. Bill was sweet and caring, always making sure I knew how much he liked me. He would send me text messages throughout the day, little notes of affection that made me feel like I was the center of his world. For a girl who had spent so much time feeling isolated and overwhelmed, this kind of attention was a lifeline. It was the first time in a long time since I felt happy like I was part of something special.

Tragically, as the weeks turned into months, the sweetness began to sour. What I initially interpreted as Bill's deep care for me started to feel more like control. His texts, once a source of joy, became incessant demands. He wanted to know where I was every minute of the day—when I got to school, when I left, who I was with. At first, I didn't think much of it. I told myself he was just being protective, that he cared about me so much that he wanted to make sure I was safe.

But it wasn't just about safety. Bill's need to know my every move started to feel oppressive. If I was even a minute late in responding to his texts, he would blow up my phone with messages, accusing me of ignoring him, of not caring about him as much as he cared about me. He would ask me to prove where I was by sending pictures or calling him to show that I wasn't lying. What started as concern quickly escalated into something much darker, a need for control that I couldn't understand or escape from.

Bill didn't stop at just monitoring my whereabouts. He began to dictate other aspects of my life as well. He would criticize my clothes, telling me what I could and couldn't wear under the guise of wanting me to look "appropriate." He didn't like it when I talked to other boys, even if it was just for school projects, and he made that very clear. He would accuse me of flirting or leading them on, even when I was simply being friendly. The more I tried to assert my independence, the tighter his grip became. He started to isolate me from my friends, subtly at first, by making me feel guilty for spending time with them instead of him. Eventually, I stopped seeing them altogether, convinced that I didn't need anyone but him.

The final straw came when I realized that Bill had people following me. His friends would watch me, reporting back to him on my every move. I remember the first time I noticed someone trailing me, a friend of Bill's who always seemed to be wherever I was. When I confronted Bill about it, he brushed it off, saying it was just a coincidence, but I knew better. The realization that I was being watched, that my every action was being scrutinized, was terrifying. I felt like a prisoner, constantly looking over my shoulder, wondering who was watching and what they were telling Bill.

At 15, I didn't have the experience or the knowledge to recognize these red flags for what they were, signs of an abusive, controlling relationship. I mistook his possessiveness for love, thinking that his demands were just signs of how much he cared about me. I was naive, desperate for affection, and completely unprepared for the emotional manipulation that Bill was subjecting me to.

As time went on, the relationship that had once made me feel special began to drain me. The constant need to report to Bill, the fear of disappointing him, the isolation from my friends, it all became too much. I was already stretched thin by the responsibilities at home, and Bill's demands pushed me to the brink. I felt like I was drowning, but I didn't know how to get out. I was too deep in, too entangled in the web of what I thought was love but was really in control.

Looking back, I wish I had never opened the door to Bill, never allowed him into my life. But at 15, I was vulnerable, starved for affection, and didn't have the tools to see through the facade. I wanted so badly to feel loved and valued, to have someone care about me, and Bill took advantage of that. What I didn't realize at the time was that love isn't about control or possessiveness—it's about respect, trust, and freedom. And what Bill offered me was the exact opposite.

One day, Bill decided to come to my house, fully aware that no one else was home. When I heard the knock on the door, I wasn't expecting it to be him. But there he stood, his expression serious, claiming that his sister was missing and asking if she was at my house. I assured him that she wasn't, that I hadn't spoken to her in days, but he didn't seem to believe me. Without waiting for an invitation, he pushed his way inside, his presence immediately filling the room with a tension that made my stomach churn.

As he walked through my home, he started accusing me of lying, insisting that I knew where his sister was. His voice grew louder and more aggressive as he checked every room and every corner, looking for something that wasn't there. The fear inside me began to grow, but so did a flicker of anger. I had been under his control for so long, but this was my home, my space, and I decided to stand up for myself.

When I finally mustered the courage to fight back, to tell him to leave, something in him snapped. Before I knew it, Bill had thrown me onto my bed, his hands pinning me down. Panic surged through me, and I screamed, begging for help, tears streaming down my face as I cried out for this nightmare to end. But no help came. No one was there to hear my screams. I was completely alone, trapped under the weight of someone I thought I knew, someone I had once trusted.

The reality of what was happening hit me like a freight train. This wasn't a nightmare I could wake up from. This was real. Bill raped me in my own home, in the place where I should have felt safest. The violation was more than physical; it shattered the very foundation of my trust, leaving me broken in a way I didn't know was possible.

Chapter: 7
From Shadows to Laughter

When it was over, I felt numb. The shock and disbelief wrapped around me like a thick fog. I didn't know what to do, where to go, or who to tell. I felt dirty, ashamed, and utterly lost. So, I stayed quiet. I kept it all inside, burying the trauma deep within me, hoping that if I didn't talk about it, maybe it would just go away. But it didn't. The pain and the memory lingered, a constant reminder of what had been taken from me.

For almost 10 years, I carried that burden alone. I didn't go to therapy, didn't turn to drugs or alcohol to numb the pain. Instead, I told myself that it happened, that I needed to woman up, stop feeling sorry for myself, and move on. Of course, moving on wasn't as simple as I tried to make it. Those years after the rape were the hardest years of my life. I was on an emotional roller coaster, fluctuating between anger, despair, and numbness that scared me. I found myself snapping at everything and everyone, the anger bubbling just beneath the surface, waiting to explode. The day I finally told my two older cousins about that nightmare is etched in my memory. I remember the way their faces changed, the way their eyes filled with tears as I recounted the horror of that day.

They didn't know what to say, and I didn't expect them to. But just saying the words out loud, finally letting the secret out after all those years, was a release I hadn't realized I needed. They hugged me as we cried together, their arms around me offering a comfort I hadn't felt in so long.

They told me I didn't deserve what happened, that it wasn't my fault, and though I had told myself those things a thousand times, hearing it from someone else made it feel real. The hard truth is that so many women have gone through the same situation as me, and many didn't survive it physically, emotionally, or mentally. But I did. I made it. I survived.

And for that, I am beyond proud of myself. I didn't let Bill consume my entire life. I didn't let him win by forcing me into a darkness I couldn't escape. I won't lie, the first 10 years were hell. I was angry, hurt, and struggling to find a way to live with the trauma. But I survived. I made it through the other side, scarred but stronger, and that's something no one can ever take away from me.

During the time my dad was in Afghanistan, my mother and I developed a weekend routine that became a cherished ritual, a way for us to bond and find some joy in the midst of all the challenges. Every Friday and Saturday night, we'd indulge in our favorite fast food, whatever we were craving that week, and settle in for a marathon of Bollywood movies. It was our little escape, our time to forget about the world outside and immerse ourselves in the colorful, dramatic, and musical world of Bollywood. We'd stay up until 2 or 3 in the morning, sitting in front of the TV, laughing, crying, and singing along with the characters on screen.

My mom had this habit of turning on the home security system every night, but she always set it in a way that made the system think no one was home. This meant that if you moved out of a certain room, the alarm would go off, assuming there was an intruder. It was a quirky little detail of our routine, something we were used to, though it did lead to some interesting moments.

One night, around 2:30 a.m., we had just finished watching one of our Bollywood movies. We were still basking in the glow of the story, the music, and the shared experience. I told my mom I was going downstairs to get some water and that I'd be right back. In my half-asleep, movie-dazed state, I completely forgot that the alarm was on. The moment I put one foot on the stairs, the alarm blared to life, shattering the peace of the night. My heart jumped into my throat as I realized what I'd done.

Panicked, I sprinted down the stairs as fast as I could to turn off the alarm, but I was too late. Within seconds, the phone rang, it was the 911 operator. I tried to stay calm as I explained that it was all just a mistake, that I had accidentally set off the alarm, and there was no emergency. The operator seemed to understand, and I thought that would be the end of it. I hung up the phone, a little shaken but relieved.

About 10 minutes later, just as I was lying back in bed next to my mom, the night erupted into chaos. We heard sirens blaring from every direction and the unmistakable sound of a helicopter circling above our house. My mom and I exchanged wide-eyed looks of disbelief. She went to the window, and what she saw made her jaw drop, we were literally surrounded by police officers. Flashing lights illuminated the dark streets, and the helicopter's spotlight swept across our yard. It looked like a scene straight out of a crime drama.

The phone rang again, and it was the police calling from the front gate. I told them once more that it was an accident, trying to convey that there was no need for all this commotion. But they insisted on checking the house, saying they couldn't leave until they were sure everything was alright. Two minutes later, there was a knock on the door. When I opened it, six police officers stood on our doorstep, asking to be let in. Behind them, I could see at least six more officers waiting outside, hands on their radios, ready to spring into action.

I kept trying to explain that it was my mistake, that there was no danger, but they were firm—they had to check the house. So, with a resigned sigh, I let them in. Two officers stayed in the dining room with my mom and me while the other four split up and began searching the house. As they moved through each room, I couldn't help but find the situation absurd. The officers were treating it like a full-blown operation, complete with backup and tactical precision. I couldn't stop laughing, especially when I heard one officer nervously call out that he was alone and needed backup.

I looked at my mom, trying to stifle my giggles, and whispered, "What does he need backup for?

No one else is in this house!" The officer's voice had a hint of fear in it, and I realized he must have been a rookie, thrown into this situation and probably imagining all sorts of scenarios. I turned to the officer standing next to me and said, "Maybe he should go downstairs for backup," before bursting into laughter. The absurdity of it all was just too much.

When the search was finally over, the officers regrouped in the dining room, clearly relieved that there was no actual emergency. They asked us what we were doing up so late, and we explained our weekend tradition of Bollywood movies and late-night snacks. As we recounted the events that had led to the alarm going off, they started to laugh too. It was contagious, the tension that had filled the house dissolved into shared laughter.

However, I could tell that the rookie officer, the one who had been so scared, wasn't amused. He had taken the situation very seriously, and now that it was all a false alarm, he seemed a bit embarrassed. But for my mom and me, it was one of the funniest things that had happened in a long time. After the police left, we climbed back into bed, still chuckling about the whole ordeal. We laughed for another hour, replaying the events in our heads, especially the rookie's panicked calls for backup. It became one of those stories we would tell and retell, a light-hearted memory amidst the challenges we were facing.

Back in high school, every other Saturday, when my mom was at work, I would turn our quiet home into the ultimate party spot. I threw the craziest kickbacks you could imagine—daytime parties that ran from 10 a.m. to 5 p.m. We were just kids, and the idea of throwing a night party was way too intimidating. But during the day, with the sun shining and the knowledge that my mom wouldn't be home until later, I felt like I could pull it off.

I would invite about 10 people over, and even though we were all teenagers, I played the perfect host, trying to emulate what I imagined adults did at their parties. I'd cook for everyone, usually pasta because it was the only thing I knew how to make decently at the time. It became my go-to dish, something I could whip up quickly and in large quantities. It was funny how seriously I took my role as the hostess, making sure everyone had enough to eat and drink, even though we were just a bunch of teenagers trying to have a good time.

Chapter: 8
Four Loko Nights and Faded Memories

My older friends would bring over Four Loko—those infamous cans that were 85%-90% proof, with the rest being flavored juice. If you don't know about the Four Loko life, let me tell you, it was intense. We'd usually share one can between two people because it would get you crazy drunk within minutes. Those things were practically a rite of passage for us back then, adding an edge to our daytime kickbacks that made them feel a little more rebellious, a little more grown-up.

The best part of these kickbacks was the basement I had turned into a game room. It was a teenager's paradise, a billiard table, a piano, a Pac-Man machine, you name it. I had everything you could think of in that game room, including a PS3 and a Nintendo 64. It was the perfect setup for hours of fun. We'd blast loud music, drink our Four Lokos, and play pool for what felt like forever. The atmosphere was electric, filled with laughter, friendly competition, and the carefree energy of youth.

Those kickbacks became some of the best memories of my high school years. Even though I don't talk to those people anymore and have no idea where they are in the world today, I still cherish those moments. They gave me a sense of freedom, a taste of what it was like to be young and reckless, even if it was just for a few hours every other Saturday.

Of course, with every wild memory comes a close call. One time, in the middle of one of our usual Saturday kickbacks, my mom called. She wasn't feeling well and told me she was coming home early. Panic set in instantly. The house was a complete mess—bottles everywhere, dishes piled up, and people still hanging out in every corner. I had no idea how I was going to get everyone out and clean up in time.

I immediately sprang into action, telling everyone to run that my mom was only 10 minutes away. The girls, sensing my desperation, started helping me clean up the house as fast as we could. I was freaking out, convinced that there was no way I wouldn't get caught this time. My heart was racing as I ran around like a madwoman, picking up bottles, washing dishes, and wiping down surfaces. It felt like a race against time, every second bringing my mom closer to the front door.

Somehow, miraculously, I managed to get everyone out of the house just in time. Two minutes later, my mom pulled into the garage. I quickly grabbed some rags, threw them on the dining table, and had the vacuum out to make it look like I had been cleaning the house for her all day.

When she walked in, I pretended I was in the bathroom, hastily wiping off the makeup I had put on for the party.

To my surprise, my mom didn't suspect a thing. She felt bad that I had spent my whole day cooking and cleaning, and at that moment, I had to stifle a laugh. I couldn't believe I had just gotten away with throwing a full-blown party without her even realizing it. It felt like I had pulled off the heist of the century. We ended up spending the rest of the evening together, eating the pasta I had cooked earlier and watching some of our favorite movies. It was a perfect end to a day that could have gone very, very wrong.

After that day, though, I decided that my kickback parties were over. The thrill of not getting caught was exhilarating, but the stress of almost getting busted wasn't worth it. I was too scared to go through that again, and I realized that the headache of pulling off a party in secret just wasn't worth it. So, I retired from my role as the hostess of wild kickbacks, content with the memories I had made and the knowledge that, somehow, I had managed to get away with it.

Loss

The loss of a person, belief, or identity has a different impact than when an object is lost. When we feel like we lose, or are forced from, our place in society or in our family, our sense of self also seems to be lost. The first time I experienced the loss of a grandparent was when my grandma on my dad's side passed away. I was so young, just a child, but that day is etched into my memory, not just because of her death but because the entire world seemed to plunge into darkness at the same time.

Loss Of Place

It was a typical morning as I got ready for school. I was having breakfast in our living room while my mom watched the news. The routine was so familiar and comforting, even until everything changed in an instant. It was around 7:00 in the morning when I noticed the television screen flash with urgent breaking news. I called out to my mom, sensing that something was terribly wrong even though I didn't fully understand it. I turned to see her face, and it was then that I saw the tears streaming down her cheeks.

The television was showing images that have since become infamous: planes crashing into the Twin Towers in New York. It was 9/11, the day that would change the world forever. Thousands of people died that day, and the shockwaves of that tragedy rippled across the globe. The atmosphere was heavy with grief and disbelief. My mom still had to go to work, but it was as if the world had come to a standstill. There was a somber silence everywhere, the kind that makes you feel like you're living in a nightmare you can't wake up from. Even the news anchors were in tears on live television, their professional facades crumbling under the weight of the horror they were reporting.

That same day, in the midst of all the chaos, my dad received a call from his father. My grandparents lived in Paris, France, so I rarely saw them unless they came to visit us, which wasn't often. I remember hearing a loud, gut-wrenching scream from my dad, a sound that sent chills down my spine. I ran to him, only to find him on the floor, crying like I had never seen before. My father, the man who was always so strong and stoic, was weeping uncontrollably, and it shook me to my core. I kept asking him if he was okay, but he couldn't speak. He was too consumed by his grief to form words.

Through his tears, he finally told me to put my shoes on because we had to walk to my aunt's house. My dad's older sister lived about three minutes away by car, but since my mom had taken the car that day, it was a 30-minute walk on foot. He held my hand as we walked, but he didn't stop crying the entire way. The silence between us was heavy, filled with the weight of his sorrow, and I felt completely helpless, not knowing how to comfort him or even understand the full extent of what was happening.

When we finally reached my aunt's house, I was met with a scene of shared grief. My aunt and cousins were in tears, holding each other and offering condolences. They kept saying, "I'm sorry for your loss," and it was then that I started crying too, even though I still didn't fully understand who had died. I felt the pain around me, the anguish in their voices, and it overwhelmed me. My dad finally told me that my grandma had passed away, and in that moment, it felt like the worst thing that could have happened.

But the horror of that day didn't end there. With 9/11 happening just hours before, everything was in chaos. The world had turned against us overnight because we were Afghan Muslims. Suddenly, we were seen as the enemy, as terrorists and the hatred was palpable. Because of the heightened security and the fear that gripped the world, my dad couldn't travel to Paris to see his mother or attend her funeral. He couldn't say goodbye or be there to bury her, and I know it tore him apart inside. I saw the pain in his eyes, the helplessness, and it broke my heart. He was forced to mourn from afar, isolated by both distance and the prejudice that had taken root in the world.

Chapter: 9
Bearing the Weight of Hatred

When I returned to school two days later, I was eager to see my classmates, hoping that being around them would bring some sense of normalcy back into my life. But I was wrong, so very wrong. The entire atmosphere at school had changed, and it wasn't just the sorrow from 9/11. It was something deeper, something darker. The other kids looked at me differently, with suspicion and hostility. Every day, I was called a terrorist. They told me my kind wasn't welcome here, that I should go back to my country, even though I was born in America. I was only 7 years old, and I couldn't understand why I was being singled out, why the kids who used to be my friends now saw me as an enemy.

It was as if the hatred their parents felt had been passed down to them, and they acted on it without hesitation. They didn't just taunt me with words; they hurt me physically too. I was beaten almost every day at school simply because of my background, because of the way I looked, because of the faith I was born into. The world had changed in an instant, and I was caught in the crossfire of its fear and anger.

One day, as I waited to be picked up from school, my dad was running late. Two girls, who had once been friendly with me, snuck up behind me and beat me so badly that my nose broke. The pain was excruciating, but what hurt more was the realization that this was my new reality. I ran to the bathroom to clean off the blood, desperate to hide the evidence before my parents saw it. At just 7 years old, I somehow managed to conceal the reason for my injury, telling my parents that I had fallen while running on the playground. They never knew the truth because I was too scared, too ashamed to tell them what was really happening at school.

That day, and the days that followed, marked the beginning of a long journey through a world that no longer felt safe. I had lost my grandmother, and in many ways, I felt like I had lost my innocence too. The grief of losing her was compounded by the hatred I faced every day, and it was a weight I carried with me for years to come.

Chapter: 10
Loss At Work

Even in my adulthood, I continue to experience racism, which I've come to understand as another form of loss, a loss of dignity, of safety, and of the basic human respect that everyone deserves. One incident that stands out vividly in my memory happened while I was working at a dental office. It was a routine day until a white male patient made it clear that he didn't want me to assist the doctor simply because I was Middle Eastern.

I remember the way he looked at me, his eyes filled with disdain. He didn't try to hide his feelings or soften his words. He demanded that the doctor either fire me or he would never return to the office again. But it wasn't just a threat to take his business elsewhere, his words carried a darker weight. He said that my kind wasn't welcome and that we should be murdered. Hearing those words, the sheer hatred in his voice sent a chill down my spine. It was a stark reminder that, despite the years that had passed since my childhood, the prejudice and ignorance that I had faced back then still existed, still thrived in the hearts of some people.

I stood there, trying to process what had just been said, a mix of anger, sadness, and disbelief swirling inside me. But before I could react, the doctor stepped in. He looked that man square in the face and, without a moment's hesitation, laughed. It wasn't the response I expected, but it was exactly what was needed. The doctor then told the man that he, too, was Middle Eastern. He made it clear that if the man wasn't happy with that, he was free to take his business elsewhere but that I was more than welcome to continue working there.

At that moment, I felt an overwhelming sense of gratitude and pride. The doctor turned to me, his expression serious, and told me something that I'd carried with me ever since. He said, "Always keep your head high and be proud of where you come from. Just because some stupid people did bad things doesn't mean we are all bad."

Those words struck a chord deep within me. They were a powerful reminder that my identity, my heritage, was something to be proud of, not something to hide or be ashamed of.

Up until that point, there had always been a part of me that hesitated, that wondered if it was safer or easier to downplay my background to avoid the potential backlash that could come from simply being who I was. But after that day, I made a decision: I would never again be afraid to tell people who I was and where I came from.

The doctor's words gave me strength, not just in that moment but in every moment since. They reminded me that ignorance and hatred, though loud and intimidating, are not insurmountable. They do not define me. My heritage, my culture, my identity, these are things to be celebrated, not hidden away.

From that day forward, I wore my identity with pride. I no longer felt the need to shrink myself or hide parts of who I was to make others more comfortable. I understood that standing tall and being proud of who I am was not just an act of defiance against the racism I encountered but a way to honor my history, my family, and my people. It was a way to reclaim the narrative, to show that despite the prejudice and hate, I would continue to stand tall, proud, and unbroken. This experience, like so many others, taught me that loss comes in many forms. But it also showed me that with every loss, there is an opportunity for growth, for resilience, and for finding strength in the face of adversity. And that is a lesson I will never forget.

Chapter: 11
Losing Del

I mostly grew up in my grandparents' house because my parents weren't well-off. They had to work 9-5 jobs, often with overtime, just to make ends meet. My godmother, who everyone called Del for short, was more than just a godmother to me, she was a second mother. I am who I am today because of her. She showered me with so much love and care, always treating me like I was her own daughter. She made sure I never felt alone, always there to comfort me, guide me, and celebrate life's little moments with me.

On my birthdays, Del made sure they were special. She would take me out, just the two of us, and we'd talk about everything, life, dreams, fears, and hopes. She had a way of making me feel understood and loved as if I were the most important person in her world. Those conversations shaped me, gave me a sense of confidence and security that I've carried with me throughout my life.

One day, however, our world turned upside down. Del sat me down, her voice heavy with the kind of seriousness I wasn't used to hearing from her. She told me she had been diagnosed with brain cancer, and it was already at Stage 3. The words hung in the air, almost unreal, like a bad dream that I couldn't wake up from. I felt utterly helpless like the ground had been pulled out from under me. It was as if I was losing another mother figure all over again, and the pain was unbearable.

The next seven months were a blur of hospital visits, chemotherapy sessions, and moments of hope mixed with fear. I watched Del fight with every ounce of strength she had, enduring the brutal effects of the treatment with a resilience that amazed me. Finally, after what felt like an eternity, we received the news we had been praying for—she was cancer-free. I remember the day we got the news. We celebrated life like never before, filled with joy and relief, thinking that we had beaten the odds, that we had more time together.

Chapter: 12
Weight of Loss and the Language of Love

But life, as it often does, had other plans. Just five months after being declared cancer-free, Del came to me with the news that her cancer had returned. This time, she said, she didn't have the strength to fight it. Hearing those words broke something inside me. I could see the toll the disease had taken on her, how it had stripped away the vibrant, strong woman I knew and loved. In her last days, she was all bones, her body a fragile shell of what it once was. It was heartbreaking to see her that way, to see how much pain she was in, and yet I tried to remain hopeful, telling her she would get better, even though deep down, I knew the truth.

The last time I saw her, I kissed her, still clinging to the hope that she would somehow pull through. I didn't know then that it would be the last time I would see her alive. Two days later, as I was getting ready to visit her, I received a call from my aunt. Her voice was thick with tears, and at that moment, I knew. I knew Del was gone. The grief hit me like a tidal wave, and I remember collapsing on the stairs, crying uncontrollably. It felt like my heart had been ripped out of my chest. I wasn't ready to lose her—I don't think I ever could have been. There was still so much I wanted to tell her, so much I wanted to share. I wanted to tell her that she was the best mother figure I could have ever asked for, that I would always be her daughter in spirit, no matter what.

That night, I went to her home, the place that had always been filled with warmth and love, and all I could see was her body lying on the floor, covered by a white sheet. The sight of it was surreal, a stark contrast to the vibrant woman I had known. When the people came to take her body away, it felt like my entire world was shattering. I had lost my best friend, my second mom, my everything. I couldn't imagine what life would be like without her. The emptiness she left behind was overwhelming, and I didn't know how I would move forward without her by my side.

In the days that followed, I feared that as time passed, I might forget her—the sound of her voice, the warmth of her smile, the way she made me feel loved. Instead, her memory has remained a constant presence in my life. Every day, I see her smile in my mind's eye, hear her laugh echoing in my thoughts. She lives on in me, in the way I carry myself, in the values she instilled in me, and in the love she gave me so freely.

I visit her grave from time to time, finding solace in those moments when I can talk to her, tell her about my life, and share what's been happening. When I'm there, I imagine her sitting under a tree in the distance, watching over me, and I feel a sense of peace that I can't find anywhere else. I still miss her so much, and I wish she could see the woman I've become. I hope she's proud of me, even with all the mistakes I've made along the way. I hope she knows that no matter how much time passes, I will always talk about her, I will always love her, and she will always be a part of me.

Chapter: 13
Loss of Ara

I was in 11th grade when my best friend Ara died in a car accident. It was one of the most devastating experiences I had to go through at such a young age. Until then, I didn't really understand what it meant to lose someone, especially a friend who was so close to me. The idea that someone you care about can just be gone, ripped away from you in an instant, was something I couldn't fully grasp. It felt impossible, like something that only happened in movies or to people far removed from my life. But suddenly, it was my reality.

I remember the day before the accident, Ara had asked me to hang out. I told him that we would plan something for the next weekend because I had to attend my cousin's bridal shower and needed to be up early. It was a simple, casual conversation, the kind we had all the time. I didn't know that when I said "next weekend," I was pushing away the last chance I would ever have to spend time with him.

The next morning, I woke up to a flood of texts and missed calls. The first one I saw simply said, "Ara is dead." That moment is still vivid in my memory like it was yesterday, my heart stopped, and I felt a cold wave of shock wash over me. I couldn't believe what I was reading.

How could Ara be dead? It didn't make any sense. I ran downstairs to the kitchen, screaming and crying, trying to make sense of it all as I told my mom what had happened. She didn't understand what was going on at first, and honestly, neither did I. The words felt foreign in my mouth, as if by saying them, I was somehow making it more real.

The days that followed were a blur of grief and disbelief. I remember going to Ara's funeral, still struggling to comprehend how someone so full of life could be gone just like that. Walking into the church, the air was thick with sorrow. All I could see was his body lying there in the casket.

He looked peaceful, almost angelic, as if he were merely sleeping. I wanted so badly to go up to him, to hug him one last time, to say goodbye. But I couldn't move. I was frozen in place, unable to take even a single step forward, with my mind racing but my body refusing to cooperate. I couldn't talk, couldn't cry, couldn't do anything but stand there, paralyzed by the sheer weight of my grief.

In that moment, I realized that I would have to learn how to live without my best friend. The thought was unbearable. Ara had been such an integral part of my life, and now I had to face the reality of a world without him in it. Fast forward to the months and years that followed—life without Ara was sad, confusing, and filled with a sense of emptiness that nothing seemed to fill. No one really knew how to handle his death, least of all me. We were all just kids trying to make sense of something that defied understanding.

Ara was buried only five minutes from my house, and for a long time, I visited him frequently. It became a ritual, a way for me to feel close to him even though he was gone. I would sit by his grave and talk to him about everything that was happening in my life, as if he were still there, listening like he always had. It brought me some comfort, knowing that I could still share my thoughts with him, even if he couldn't respond.

Unfortunately, as the years went by, I found myself visiting less and less. I stopped going on holidays, birthdays, and even on the anniversary of his death. It wasn't that I had forgotten about him, how could I? Ara's memory was etched into my heart, and I carried him with me every day. But I felt like I had to move on with my life, to accept that death is a part of life, even when it takes someone too soon.

For a long time, I struggled with guilt for not visiting Ara's grave as often as I used to. This is another lesson I never wanted to learn when I realized that moving on doesn't mean forgetting. It doesn't mean I loved him any less or that his memory means any less to me. I had to find a way to keep living, even with the pain of his loss, because grief is not something that ever truly goes away. It changes over time, becomes a part of who you are, but it never fully leaves you.

For the first time in my life, I came to understand that death doesn't wait for the right time. It doesn't care about age or your plans for the future. It comes when it comes, and all we can do is learn to live with the loss, for life is fragile, and we must cherish the moments we have with the people we love.

As I got older, I experienced so many sudden deaths that I eventually became numb to the pain. Since life doesn't stop, even when it feels like your world is crumbling, I had learned, perhaps out of necessity, to compartmentalize it, to push it aside so I could keep moving forward. It wasn't that I stopped caring or that the losses didn't affect me, they did. But after a while, it was like my heart had built a protective barrier around itself, a way to cope with the relentless waves of grief that seemed to follow me. I didn't grieve like most people do. For me, the tears would come in a rush, overwhelming and intense, but they never lasted long. I'd cry for two hours, maybe less, and then I'd wipe my eyes, take a deep breath, and go about my day as if nothing had happened.

When it's time for the memorial services, though, then I am different. That's when everything I'd been holding back would come pouring out. In that space, surrounded by others who were also grieving, I allowed myself to feel the full weight of my sorrow. I would cry, sometimes uncontrollably, as if all the grief I'd been suppressing finally had a place to be expressed.

But even in those moments, I never saw death as a final goodbye, I always told myself that it was more of an "I'll see you later." It is a reimagining of the situation that I have kept over the years, my way of coping, of surviving the pain that comes with losing the people you love. It allowed me to find joy and purpose. It was the only way I could bear the constant ache of grief gnawing at me, to keep the tears from rolling down my face every time I thought about my absent loved ones. I simply pretended that the people who had passed away were just on a long vacation, far away, somewhere out of reach where there was no cell phone service, and weren't really gone forever. This allows me to hold on to a sense of connection to them in their absence. I imagined that one day, when their "trip" was over, we'd be reunited, and everything would be okay again.

Now, whenever I face another loss, I would remind myself that it isn't goodbye. It is simply an "I'll see you later." I allow myself to remember the good times, to cherish the memories without being consumed by the sadness of their passing. It is how I managed to keep going, even when it felt like the world was asking too much of me. I know that everyone grieves differently, and my way might not make sense to others. But for me, it's what works. It's how I've learned to navigate the pain of loss and keep my heart intact. Because in the end, I believe that love doesn't die with the people we lose, it just waits for the day when we can say "hello" again.

Chapter: 14
Let's talk about love...

Growing up, love was a concept that seemed distant and almost forbidden. In my household, friendships were heavily monitored, and the idea of having guy friends was completely out of the question. My parents, especially my father, were very strict, enforcing rules that left little room

for the typical social interactions that most kids my age took for granted. The idea of casually mentioning a crush or introducing a boyfriend to my parents was something I couldn't even fathom. In fact, I don't think I ever told my parents about any guy in my life until I was 28 years old.

For those who aren't familiar with Afghan culture, this might sound extreme, maybe even shocking. But for me, it was my reality. Being an only child in an Afghan family comes with its own set of expectations and pressures, and strictness is often at the center of it. Even now, as an adult, I still find myself adhering to some of the same rules that governed my life as a teenager. For example, I still ask for permission to go out, and if I'm allowed to go out one night, I know I won't be allowed to go out the next night. It's a balance I've had to strike to maintain peace at home, but it's also a reflection of the deeply ingrained values and traditions that have shaped my life.

Love, in this context, becomes something you tiptoe around, something you learn to experience quietly, often in secret. The idea of openly dating or bringing someone home was out of the question. Love wasn't something to be explored freely, it was something to be carefully considered, often with the approval and oversight of family. This meant that any romantic feelings I had were often internalized, kept private, and shared only with close friends who understood the cultural boundaries I was navigating.

As I got older, those boundaries didn't completely disappear, but I learned how to navigate them more effectively. By the time I was 28, I had finally reached a point where I felt comfortable enough to talk to my parents about a guy in my life. It wasn't easy, and even then, the conversation was approached with caution and a deep awareness of the cultural expectations that still loomed large in our household.

Looking back, I realize that my experience with love has been shaped as much by cultural norms as by my own feelings. The way I've learned to approach relationships, carefully, thoughtfully, and often with a sense of responsibility, reflects the balance I've had to maintain between my desires and the expectations placed on me. It's a delicate dance, one that many in my community will understand, and one that has taught me a lot about patience, understanding, and the different ways love can manifest in a life shaped by tradition.

Chapter: 15
Love is…Henry?

When I was 28 years old, I experienced my first real love, a mysterious, handsome man who seemed to embody everything I had ever dreamed of. His name was Henry, an Egyptian man who captured my heart in ways I never expected. Like a scene out of a romantic movie, I thought I had found my happily ever after. But, as life often teaches us, things are rarely as simple as they seem.

Henry was around my height, with a demeanor that exude masculinity without being overbearing. He wasn't the buff, gym-obsessed type, but rather, he had an average build that suited him perfectly. His face was undeniably handsome, but what made him even more attractive was his presence, something about the way he carried himself made him irresistibly sexy. He was everything I could have ever imagined in a partner. He was my person, or at least I thought he was.

Henry was an enigma, a man who was hardheaded and emotionless on the surface, yet beneath that exterior, he was incredibly caring. We met in the most unexpected way, after I had a terrible accident and was desperately searching for a lawyer. Henry saw one of my Instagram posts about the situation and, out of nowhere, reached out to refer me to his lawyer. I remember thinking, "Wow, this man is so thoughtful," and that simple act of kindness sparked something between us.

As the months passed, Henry and I grew closer, and I began to feel like I had finally found someone I could truly connect with. He was a private person, someone who didn't easily let others into his life. It felt special, knowing that he trusted me enough to share parts of his world with me. But just as I was starting to settle into the idea of us, I discovered something that caught me off guard.

Henry had children, something I was aware of early on. But what I didn't know was that he had more than one. In fact, he had four children. When I first found out, I could almost hear the collective voice of my friends and family in my head saying, "Girl, that is the biggest red flag right there." But in my heart, I didn't see it that way. Henry's private nature meant that he only shared things when he felt he could trust someone completely, and I respected that. I didn't see his children as a red flag but rather as a part of his life that he was slowly revealing to me as we grew closer.

Looking back, it's easy to see how others might have viewed this as a warning sign, but at the time, all I saw was a man who was complicated, guarded, and trying to protect the people he cared about. I was willing to accept that and move forward with him despite the uncertainties. Because when you're in love, you often see what you want to see, and I wanted to believe that Henry was the one.

Getting to know someone truly takes time, and in the beginning, I didn't expect Henry to reveal his entire life story to me. After all, we weren't officially dating at first, so it made sense that certain details would unfold gradually. As time went on, Henry and I grew closer, and our conversations naturally turned to topics like marriage and starting a family. Those discussions filled me with excitement, imagining a future together where we would build a life as partners.

I remember one particular argument we had about weddings. Unlike most women who dream of a big, elaborate ceremony, I was content with the idea of just having a small party. To me, a wedding was more about the commitment than the spectacle. But Henry had different ideas. He wanted a big wedding, at least 1,000 guests, because his first wedding had only 500 people, and he had always dreamed of something grander. Henry had this all-or-nothing approach when it came to hosting events; it was either big and bold, or it wasn't worth doing at all. And honestly, I loved that about him.

His enthusiasm for going all out was one of the things that made him so charismatic.

We even talked about potential names for our future children. I had a list of names I loved, and after rejecting most of them, Henry surprisingly agreed to the name "Noura." I knew it wasn't his favorite, but I could tell he was just trying to make me happy—and it worked. I would get so excited every time Henry called me. It felt like the world around me froze, and all that mattered were our conversations, even if they were brief. He would check up on me every night before heading to work, a small gesture that showed me just how much he cared.

Henry played a significant role in boosting my confidence. He encouraged me not to let things bother me as much as they used to, helping me develop a thicker skin. But despite all the good, there was one major issue I couldn't shake, Henry was incredibly secretive. It often felt like I was playing a guessing game, trying to piece together the truth from the bits he was willing to share. And when I did ask questions, I couldn't shake the feeling that he wasn't telling me everything. His stories never seemed to add up, and it was frustrating.

For example, the entire time I was with Henry, I believed he was divorced and no longer living with his wife. But almost a year into our relationship, his own best friends revealed that he was still living with his wife and their children. I was beyond heartbroken. I couldn't believe I had been deceived for so long, believing every word Henry had told me. I had even shared the news about him with my family, who, despite never meeting him, loved him because they saw how ' happy he made me.

Chapter: 16
Space Between

I always believed that Henry loved me in his own way, but he was a puzzle I could never fully solve. The mystery surrounding him only made me more obsessed. Every day, I discovered something new about him, like the fact that he didn't like sweets or baseball, yet he supported his older son by taking him to all his little league games. That was another thing I deeply admired about Henry—his love for his children. He wasn't perfect to me, and he treated me horribly at times, but as a father, he was exceptional. I used to think, "Wow if only every man could be like him when it comes to fatherhood."

One thing I really respected about Henry was how he handled conflicts. No matter how angry I got, no matter how much I yelled or cussed him out—and believe me, I did that plenty of times—he never responded in kind. He never cussed me out or called me names. Instead, he would listen, let me vent, and then calmly apologize. Even though Henry was stubborn and rarely admitted he was wrong, with me, he was different. He couldn't stand seeing me upset or in tears, so he would apologize, even if it felt half-hearted at times. He made sure to show that he cared, and that meant the world to me.

I remember one day when we were out at a public event, surrounded by the buzz of people and laughter, when I suddenly felt an overwhelming wave of sickness wash over me. It hit out of nowhere, like a storm I never saw coming. My head started spinning, my vision blurred, and I could feel the strength draining from my body.

Henry immediately noticed the change in me. His eyes widened with worry, and without hesitation, he pulled me away from the crowd, his hand gripping mine tightly as if he were afraid I might collapse. He led me to a quieter area, away from the noise and chaos, his arm wrapped protectively around my waist. I could feel his breath quickening against my shoulder, his voice calm but urgent as he asked me over and over, "Are you okay? What's happening?"

I had never seen him so scared. There was a franticness in his gaze, and I could see the fear he was trying to hide. He was doing everything he could to keep me from ending up in the hospital. He wrapped me in his arms, holding me close, his lips pressing against my forehead as he whispered, "Everything's going to be okay. I've got you."

Henry thought it was an anxiety attack, and maybe it was, I had no idea what was happening to me. All I knew was that my fingers were turning a strange shade of blue and purple, and I could hardly feel them. It was like they had gone numb, disconnected from the rest of my body. When I tried to speak, my voice betrayed me, stuttering and slurring until the words turned into a jumbled mess. No matter how hard I tried, I couldn't get a single coherent word out, and tears started to stream down my face. I felt trapped inside myself, unable to communicate, while panic spread through my veins like ice.

Henry's face grew more worried with every passing second, his brow furrowed deeply. He begged me to let him take me to the hospital, but I shook my head, too frightened to move. So, he sat with me on the curb, pulling me into his chest, his arms tight around me as if he could somehow shield me from whatever was happening. He kept kissing my head, whispering soothing words, trying to calm the tremors in my body. I could feel his heart racing against my cheek, a steady, rapid thrum that betrayed how scared he truly was. But he kept a brave face, for my sake. He stayed with me for hours, holding me close until I began to feel the life returning to my limbs, the coldness in my fingers gradually fading. Even after I assured him I was okay, he refused to leave. Later that night, he called me several times to check on me, his voice soft but insistent, asking if I needed anything if I was still feeling alright. He was relentless in his concern, refusing to sleep until he was sure I was okay.

That night changed something in me. As I lay in bed, listening to his voice on the phone, I realized just how deeply I had fallen for him. I realized I wanted to spend forever with this man who cared for me in a way no one ever had. I remember very clearly the time I kept a secret from Henry for a whole month because I was terrified of how he might react. It wasn't just any secret, it was something deeply personal, something I wasn't sure how he would handle. I felt a mixture of fear and shame, and the thought of telling him weighed heavily on me every day. We had grown so close, and I didn't want to ruin what we had, but the secret was eating away at me.

I remember very clearly the time I held a secret from Henry for an entire month. I was terrified of how he might react, so I kept it buried deep inside, too afraid to bring it to light. The weight of that secret pressed down on me every day, and it wasn't just any secret, it was something that struck at the core of who I was and the darkness I was battling.

One evening, as we lay together, lost in one of those deep conversations that seemed to make the rest of the world fade away, I felt the need to tell him. The guilt had been gnawing at me, and I couldn't keep it from him any longer. I turned to him and quietly said, "I'm sorry." He looked at me, confusion etched on his face, and asked why I was apologizing. His expression was a mixture of concern and curiosity as if he was bracing himself for whatever it was I was about to reveal.

With a heavy heart, I told him that I had been hiding something from him, something that I hadn't been able to share out of fear of how he might react. His face remained blank, his eyes searching mine, trying to figure out what could be so terrible that I had kept it from him for so long. The silence between us grew thick, the air heavy with anticipation and dread.

Finally, I gathered the courage to confess. I told Henry that two days before my birthday, I had tried to slit my wrist in the bathtub to end my life. As the words left my mouth, I saw the color drain from his face. His eyes, usually so guarded, filled with tears. It was a look I will never forget, a mixture of shock, pain, and a deep, profound sadness. Without hesitation, he pulled me down into his arms, holding me as tightly as he could, as if trying to shield me from the world, from myself. He didn't say anything at first, just held me, letting the weight of what I had just confessed sink in. I could feel his heart beating against mine, strong and steady, a stark contrast to the turmoil I had been feeling.

When he finally spoke, his voice was thick with emotion. He made me swear that I would never do it again, ever. "Promise me," he said, his voice barely above a whisper, "promise me that if you ever feel that way again, you'll call me right away. No matter what time it is, no matter where I am, just call me." I could see how desperate he was for me to make that promise, to give him some assurance that he wouldn't lose me to the darkness I had been battling alone.

That day, everything changed for me. Up until that moment, I had seen Henry as a strong, caring man, but now he became something more, he became my fireplace. The kind of warmth that envelopes you on a cold, dark night, the kind of love that makes you feel safe and protected, even when the world outside is harsh and unforgiving. He was the place I could go to when everything else seemed too much to bear, the person who could hold me together when I felt like I was falling apart.

Even as I found comfort in his arms, a part of me knew that not every love story has a happy ending. Life is unpredictable, and no matter how much love you share, it doesn't always conquer all. Still, in that moment, as I lay in his embrace, I felt something I hadn't felt in a long time, hope. Hope that maybe, just maybe, this love could be the one to last. But as life often reminds us, love, no matter how powerful, can't always change the course of fate.

Henry had one major flaw that I couldn't ignore: he often let everyone get in his ears about me, and because these people were his friends for many years, he tended to believe what they said. It was frustrating because, despite the deep connection we shared, there was always this lingering doubt that others could so easily sway him.

Let's rewind a bit. During the holidays, I decided to take a mini trip with some friends to Palm Desert. It was supposed to be a brief escape from the pressures of everyday life, a chance to unwind and forget about the stresses that had been weighing me down. But the trip quickly turned into a nightmare. One night, after we had all been drinking, a fight broke out between me and one of my friends. The cause? I had caught her in the bathroom with a man I had been talking to. It wasn't anything serious with him, just casual conversations, but it felt like a deep betrayal that she would go behind my back like that. In that moment, she instantly became an ex-friend.

At the time, Henry and I were on a break. Like any relationship, we had our ups and downs, and this was one of those rough patches. The man I had been talking to wasn't significant to me, but it was the principle of the matter—my friend had crossed a line, and that hurt. But what happened next took things to a level I could never have imagined.

In the heat of the argument, the man put his hands on me. He didn't just push me away or try to calm the situation, he beat me. The blows came so fast and so hard that at one point, I blacked out. When I came to, I was lying on the kitchen floor with blood running down my face. My body was in shock, and I couldn't comprehend how this had happened to me. I remember thinking, "How could this happen to me? How could a man put his hands on me like this?" It was as if I was reliving all the pain from my past, but this time, it was a stranger who had inflicted the damage.

You would think that having grown up with violence, I might have been desensitized to it. But the truth is, no matter how many times it happens, it never gets easier. The shock, the fear, the betrayal, they were all there, raw and overwhelming. In my dazed state, I tried to call Henry, but he didn't answer. I was alone at that moment, trying to process what had just happened to me. I decided to sleep it off, thinking that maybe, by morning, things would somehow make more sense. But Mr. No Name had taken the car keys and my wallet, trapping me in a situation that felt increasingly dangerous.

I woke up the next day around 7 am, while everyone else was still asleep. My body ached, and I could feel the bruises starting to form. I knew I had to get out of there. I quietly searched for my belongings, found the car keys and my wallet, and then I ran, literally ran, for my life. I called my best friend, desperate for help, and asked her to meet me somewhere safe. I was two hours away from home, but I just needed to see someone who made me feel secure, someone who wouldn't hurt me.

My best friend came to my rescue, and as soon as I saw her, I broke down. She didn't ask questions; she just made sure I was okay. But she also knew that I needed to tell Henry what had happened. She forced me to call him to explain everything. When Henry answered the phone, I could hear the concern in his voice even before I started speaking. As I told him about the assault, about waking up on the kitchen floor with blood running down my face, he didn't hesitate. He asked if I was okay and told me to go to the hospital immediately.

The next day, Henry came to see me. When he saw the bruises and scars on my body, I could see the anger in his eyes. He was livid, but not at me, at the man who had hurt me. He told me not to worry about anything, that he would take care of everything. At that moment, I knew Henry was my safe place. Despite the ups and downs, despite the times we were on a break or struggling to understand each other, I knew I could always count on him. He was the one person who, no matter where life took us, would always be there for me.

This experience solidified something I had always felt but maybe hadn't fully realized until then, Henry was more than just a lover; he was my protector. And in a world that often felt so unpredictable and cruel, knowing that I had someone like Henry in my corner meant everything to me.

Fast forward two months after I had opened up to Henry about my suicidal attempt. I went to our favorite restaurant, thinking it would be like any other day, a chance for us to connect and enjoy each other's company. But as soon as I walked in, I could tell something was very wrong. Henry was there, but instead of the warm, comforting presence I was used to, he was radiating anger.

His eyes, which once looked at me with so much care, were now filled with something dark, something cold. It was as if he wanted to lash out as if all his anger was directed at me, and I had no idea why.

I asked to sit next to him, hoping to ease whatever tension was there, but the look he gave me like I didn't even have the right to speak to him, was chilling. It was as if all the love and warmth he had ever shown me had vanished, replaced by something harsh and unforgiving. I couldn't understand what had happened. Days went by, and we continued to see each other almost every day. Each time, I hoped he would eventually open up and tell me what was bothering him, but he never did. He just kept his distance, emotionally shut off from me, while I was left in the dark.

Then, one day, everything changed. I realized Henry had blocked me on everything, his phone, social media, and every way we had to communicate. It was like I had been completely erased from his life. The man I loved, my fireplace, my protector, my best friend, he was gone. And not just gone, but acting as if I had never meant anything to him, as if I was just another piece of trash to be discarded.

For three long months, I lived in this state of not knowing. The worst part wasn't just the loss; it was the lack of understanding, the lack of knowing what had gone so horribly wrong. I would see Henry, and he would walk past me like I didn't even exist. It was as if all the memories, all the moments we shared, had been wiped clean from his mind. The silence, the complete and utter disregard, was more painful than any argument we could have had.

I kept asking myself, "What did I do wrong? What could have caused this?" But I never got an answer. And that unknown, that gnawing question, was what hurt the most. I wished he would just tell me, explain what I had done to deserve this treatment, but he never did. Instead, he just acted like I was nobody like I had never been someone he cared for.

Chapter: 17
Silent Walls

As time went by, I started to realize something painful yet important: if Henry truly loved or cared for me, he would have tried to fix whatever the issue was. He would have communicated, would have given me the chance to understand, and maybe even made amends. But he didn't.

Our pride, his, mine, maybe both, got in the way, and it cost us everything. The love we had, or what I thought we had, crumbled because neither of us could break through that wall of silence and pride.

Later, I discovered that the reason Henry had been so upset and distant was due to some rumors he had heard about me. At first, I couldn't believe that he would allow baseless gossip to come between us, especially after everything we had shared. I knew those rumors were complete bullshit, fabrications from people who had no real understanding of our relationship. But despite knowing the truth, I didn't have the energy or the courage to confront him about it. I was already exhausted from months of trying to figure out what had gone wrong, and the thought of another confrontation felt unbearable. So, I made the difficult choice to let him be and started to move on with my life, as I've always done when faced with difficult situations.

Moving on from Henry wasn't easy. He had been such a significant part of my life, someone who helped me grow as a person. He taught me not to let negative energy or toxic people influence my happiness. For a long time, he was the person who made me feel safe, my fireplace in a cold world. But as much as it hurt, I knew I had to let him go. Holding onto someone who believed in rumors rather than trusting me, someone who kept secrets and shut me out wasn't going to help me move forward.

Even though I've tried to move on, Henry still crosses my path. We both love going to the same restaurant, and it's almost inevitable that we run into each other a couple of times a week. When we do, there's this unspoken tension, a glance here, a look there, but nothing more. It's strange, seeing someone who was once so close to you now feels like a stranger. But despite the hurt, I know my worth, and I know that I had to let him go. It's a painful realization but necessary for my own growth and well-being.

What hurts the most, though, is the lies. Recently, I found out that Henry had a vasectomy and had hidden it from me from day one. It was like a punch in the gut. I couldn't understand why he kept talking to me about having a family when, in reality, that was something we could never have without medical intervention. It made me question everything, whether he ever truly loved me or if he just liked the idea of me. It felt like he had a motive from the very beginning, and while I had believed he loved me, I'm no longer sure that was the case. Maybe he was just attracted to the idea of what we could be without ever really wanting anything more than that. Looking back, there were so many red flags I ignored. Henry never wanted to go out, always coming up with excuses for why he didn't want to go to dinner or do anything outside the house. I accepted his reasons because I loved him, even though deep down, I knew something wasn't right. We had gotten to know each other well in some ways, but in others, we were practically strangers. He didn't know my favorite food, flowers, or movies, and I didn't know his. You'd think that knowing these small details would be important when you're with someone, but I've come to realize that it's not about those superficial things. It's about getting to know someone's personality, understanding how they treat you, and recognizing whether they truly care for you. That, to me, is far more important than knowing their favorite movie.

In the end, Henry will always be a part of my life, but not in the way I once imagined. He's a chapter in my story, one that taught me valuable lessons about love, trust, and self-worth. And while it hurts to let go, I know it's the right thing to do. I deserve someone who truly loves me for who I am, not just the idea of me.

One thing I've learned from this entire experience is, honestly, FUCK LOVE. When there are red flags, you have to open your eyes and take action, nothing and no one is worth losing your sanity over. Unfortunately, I allowed Henry to consume my life, to toy with my emotions, and to break me into a million pieces. We see each other almost daily, and it's so hard not to go over and snap at him, to demand answers. I want to ask him why he did what he did to me. What was his purpose? Why did he fill my head with lies? I never hurt him; I always had his back and respected him more than anything in this world. But now I realize it was a one-way love, and that realization is devastating.

People always say that men will come back, no matter how much time has passed or how much anger there is—they always try to find a way back into your life. I thought I was finally over Henry; I was beginning to heal, and then, about five months later, he decided he wanted to have a sit-down conversation with me. Out of the blue, he reached out, waiting all day to text Mina and me, asking us to meet him and talk. I wasn't ready for that. I didn't know what to expect or how the conversation was going to go. As soon as he sat down, my body tensed up. I was bracing myself for a fight, ready to let all my anger out, but I told myself that I wasn't going to give him the satisfaction of seeing me lose control. I wasn't going to let Henry get the best of me or react to whatever nonsense was about to come out of his mouth.

When he started talking, I couldn't even look him in the face. I just sat there, listening to the garbage spewing out of his mouth. He started by saying that his phone had been ringing nonstop, and people were complaining about me. Seriously? I thought. Like, bitch, please, you're not that important for me to be running my mouth about you. Instead of explaining what his issue with me was and how we could possibly fix it, he just wanted us both to stop talking about each other. I agreed, telling him that I didn't care what anyone had to say or think about me. But deep down, his words cut deep. Henry then gave me a half-hearted, fake apology, not even understanding why I was so upset. How can you apologize when you don't know about the sleepless nights I endured? The nights when I wanted to end my life again because of the pain he caused? How did I fall back into a deep depression and have to claw my way out of it all over again after I thought I had healed?

I sat there, trying to speak, trying to let out the scream that was building inside me, but nothing came out. I wanted to cuss him out, to lay into him for everything he had done, but I couldn't. The only thing I managed to ask him about was his lies. He admitted that he was, in fact, still with his wife, and he showed no remorse. You would think that he might feel some guilt, some regret, but no, there was nothing. I sat there, pouring out my heart, telling him how he had destroyed me, how he had shattered my heart into countless pieces. But as I looked into his eyes, all I saw was a blank stare, as if he didn't understand the depth of the pain he had caused me.

He had filled my head with so much bullshit, and for what? A good time? Why couldn't he have been honest from the start about his intentions? When I confronted him about his wife, all he could say was, "All men are dogs," as if that was a valid excuse. Are you kidding me? You cheated on your wife and allowed people to think I was a homewrecker for months. How could you do that to an innocent person? In the end, he offered another hollow apology for the pain he had caused, but it didn't feel sincere. It felt like he was just going through the motions, not truly understanding or caring about the damage he had done.

As I sat there, I couldn't help but question everything. Did he ever love or care for me? Was it all just a game to him? Was anything in our relationship even real? We left that conversation with a superficial sense of closure as if we had both agreed to move on with our lives. But the truth is, I only looked at him twice during that entire conversation. The rest of the time, I couldn't bear to look at him because I knew I would break down and cry my eyes out. When Mina and I left, I had a full-blown meltdown in the parking garage. I felt so disgusted, not just with Henry, but with myself for ever letting him into my life. I felt sorry for his wife, for the lies she was living, and for the role I had unknowingly played in it all.

I felt used and betrayed on so many levels. I didn't know how I could ever trust anyone again after what Henry did to me. The road to healing is long, and I know it will take time. But that's okay. I'm giving myself permission to take all the time I need to heal. One day, I hope to wake up and realize that I'm finally over Henry, that he no longer has any power over me, and that he doesn't affect my life in any way. That will be the day I know I've truly moved on.

After that conversation with Henry, I went home, but I couldn't shake the feeling that I was left with more questions than answers. I tried to process everything he said, but nothing seemed to settle in my mind. I wasn't satisfied. There were things I needed to know, things I couldn't let go of. The next day, I went to our favorite spot, the place where we used to hang out together. And

there he was—Henry, sitting on the couch, acting like he was El Chapo. Yes, I called him El Chapo because, for some reason, everyone seems to be scared of him when he's upset. But to me, Henry was harmless, and it always made me laugh when people talked about how intimidating he was.

I wanted to say something, but the words just wouldn't come out. I thought we had agreed to be cordial, to be civil with each other, but when we saw each other, neither of us said a word. It was like we were both too proud, too hurt, to acknowledge each other. We just acted like we didn't care, like the other person didn't exist. But I couldn't let it go. I waited until the end of the day, hoping for a chance to talk to Henry and get some clarity. When I saw that he had unblocked me on his phone, I sent him a message asking if we could have a private conversation.

We met in the back, away from everyone else, and sat at a table. I could feel the tears welling up, but I held them back as hard as I could. I had to ask him, point blank, "Did you ever love me like you claimed to?" I needed to hear it from him to see if there was any truth to the words he had

once said to me. Henry looked me straight in the eyes and said, "Yes." And in that moment, I felt it. I felt how much it hurt him that he had hurt me, and that I would even question his love for me.

He reassured me that he was never with his wife while he and I were together but that he had to get back with her for personal reasons. It wasn't what I wanted to hear, but I respected his decision. It's his life, and as much as it hurt me to the core, there was nothing I could do about it. Henry told me that he wasn't worth my tears, but he didn't know that I would give my life for him in a heartbeat. Yes, I would literally jump in front of a bullet for him or give him my kidney if, God forbid, anything like that happened. I accepted everything about Henry, never questioning his life or his choices because, in my heart, he was and forever will be the Clyde to my Bonnie.

After that conversation, something shifted between us. We started talking again like we used to in the good old days, laughing and catching up on life. I realized how much I had missed him, his laugh, his presence. Who knows what the future holds, but I truly am happy for him. I want him to make things right with his family. I want nothing but good things for him. I don't know what the future holds for Henry, but I do know one thing: he has my back, no matter what. We both need to get better at communicating with each other, but I believe we'll find a way.

Ever since Henry and I started talking again, I've been having dreams about him almost every night. I can never quite figure out the meaning of these dreams. Most of the time, they're beautiful, so real that I don't want to wake up. But other times, they're nightmares, the kind that makes me jump out of bed, covered in sweat. I don't know what these dreams mean or what they're trying to tell me. Henry is always on my mind, and I often wonder if he's truly happy in his life. But I know I have no right to ask him that or to get involved in any way. It's something I have to come to terms with, just like everything else.

Chapter: 18
You're the one who held me up

To Henry:

If you're reading this, I want you to know that you'll always have a place in my heart, even though things didn't turn out the way I had hoped between us. Despite everything, there's a part of me that will always care for you that will always remember the good times we shared. I've come to terms with the fact that our relationship didn't end the way I wanted, but I've also realized that I can't hold onto bitterness. I've decided to forgive you because I understand that life is complicated, and sometimes, we make choices that hurt the people we care about, even if that was never our intention.

I'll always be here if you ever need anything, no matter how much time has passed. If life ever brings us back together, just know that I've forgiven you because I understand the pressures you were under and the reasons behind your actions. I'm still learning, still working on trying to rebuild the trust that was broken between us. It's not easy, but I'm committed to the process because I know that you meant something special to me, and I want to hold onto that, even if it's just in the form of a memory.

I love you more than anything, and I truly wish that life had given us a real chance to be together. I've always believed that we could have been great, that we had the potential to build something beautiful together. But sometimes, life doesn't work out the way we want it to, and we have to accept that. Still, I hope you succeed in everything you set out to do. I want you to accomplish all your goals, find happiness, and to be the amazing man I always knew you were.

If another woman comes into your life, I hope you treat her with the love and respect she deserves. Be honest with her from the start, make your intentions clear, and avoid the heartache and drama that we went through. It's not worth it, Henry. The pain and confusion that come from mixed signals and hidden truths can tear someone apart, and I wouldn't wish that on anyone.

There's a song that always reminds me of you, and yes, it's super cheesy, but it's the one thing that helped me hold onto the love I had for you during our hardest days. It's "Because You Loved Me" by Celine Dion. The lyrics speak to how I felt about you, how much your support meant to me, even when things were tough:

For all those times you stood by me,
For all the truth that you made me see,
For all the joy you brought to my life,
For all the wrong that you made right,
For every dream you made come true,
For all the love I found in you,
I'll be forever thankful, baby.

You're the one who held me up,
Never let me fall.
You're the one who saw me through,
Through it all.
You were my strength when I was weak,
You were my voice when I couldn't speak.
You were my eyes when I couldn't see;
You saw the best there was in me.
Lifted me up when I couldn't reach,
You gave me faith 'cause you believed.
I'm everything I am
Because you loved me.

That song encapsulates everything I felt, the gratitude I had for you during the good times and the strength you gave me when I needed it most. Even though things didn't work out, I want you to know that I'm grateful for the time we had together. You were my strength, my voice, my eyes when I couldn't see clearly, and I'll always cherish that.

So, Henry, as we both move forward with our lives, I want you to remember that you were loved deeply, even if things didn't end the way we wanted. I hope you find peace, happiness, and fulfillment in everything you do. And if our paths ever cross again, I hope we can look back on our time together with fondness rather than pain.

Love, The woman you broke.

Love is…James?

Four months went by after the rollercoaster with Henry, and during that time, I reconnected with an old friend named Jake. When Jake hit me up, I was a bit surprised—after all, we didn't part ways on the best of terms. There was tension and hurt that had built up over time, but when he reached out, it was clear that he wanted to make things right. He apologized sincerely for his past mistakes, and I could see that he was genuinely trying to make amends. The thing about me is that I have a big heart, and no matter how much someone might hurt me, I find it hard to hold a grudge. Forgiveness is something that comes naturally to me, maybe because I believe that we're all human and we all mess up. I've made my share of mistakes too, and I would want someone to forgive me if I ever hurt them.

Chapter: 19
Unpredictability of Fate

So, I forgave Jake, and slowly, we started rebuilding our friendship. I could tell he was a changed man, more thoughtful and considerate than before. One day, out of the blue, Jake called me on FaceTime, and when I answered, I noticed he wasn't alone. There was someone else on the call with him, and as the screen adjusted, I saw this incredibly handsome guy sitting next to him. My heart did a little flip, okay, a big flip, when I realized that this friend of Jake's was Afghan.

There was something about him that just drew me in immediately. From the moment I saw him, I thought to myself, I need to know who this guy is and what he's all about. I couldn't help but ask Jake to put in a good word for me, even though I felt like a giddy teenager all over again.

A couple of days later, Jake invited me to bring Starbucks to their office. It was a casual request, but I knew the real reason, he wanted me to meet his cousin, the handsome man from the FaceTime call. I remember walking into the office with the drinks, my heart pounding in my chest. I was excited but also incredibly nervous. This guy, who I later learned was named James, was exactly my type—charming, polite, and drop-dead gorgeous. But as luck would have it, when I arrived, James was in a meeting. I didn't want to interrupt, so I quietly left the drinks on the table and slipped out of the office.

As I walked back to my car, my nerves were still on high alert. I couldn't believe how jittery I felt, like a high schooler with a crush. Five minutes after I left the office, my phone buzzed with a FaceTime call from a number I didn't recognize. Curious, I decided to answer, and to my surprise, it was James on the other end of the line. He had finished his meeting, noticed I had left, and wanted to introduce himself properly. "Hi," he said with a warm smile that made my heart skip a beat. "I'm so sorry I couldn't introduce myself in person, but I just got done with my meeting and saw that you had left. I wanted to say thank you for bringing drinks to the office. By the way, my name is James."

I could feel the heat rising in my cheeks as I tried to keep my cool. But there was no hiding it—I was blushing like crazy, probably turning the brightest shade of tomato you could imagine. I stumbled through my words, trying to sound casual, but inside I was freaking out. James was even more charming and kind than I had imagined, and the fact that he had taken the time to call me back just to introduce himself made my heart melt.

From that moment on, I knew that there was something special about James. I had never really believed in love at first sight, but meeting him made me question everything I thought I knew about love. There was a connection, an undeniable spark, and I couldn't wait to see where things would go from here.

From this moment, James and I were inseparable. It felt like we had known each other forever, even though it had only been a few days. We would FaceTime for hours on end, losing track of time as we shared stories, laughed, and got to know each other on a deeper level. It was as if the universe had aligned to bring us together, and neither of us wanted to waste a single moment.

Every conversation felt effortless, every laugh genuine, and with each passing day, I found myself falling more and more in love with him.

What made it even more special was that I met James just four days before his 39th birthday. Normally, birthdays are a big deal, and people tend to spend them with those they've known for a long time. But James wanted to celebrate his with me. On the day of his birthday, he took time off work just to have lunch with me. We decided to meet at a cozy hookah lounge, a place that felt intimate yet relaxed. My best friend joined us, and the three of us shared drinks, stories, and so much laughter.

I was honestly head over heels for James, not just because he was incredibly handsome, though that certainly didn't hurt, but because he had this amazing sense of humor that could light up any room. His jokes weren't just funny; they were the kind that would make you laugh so hard you'd cry, and it was clear that he enjoyed making people happy. That day at the hookah lounge was one of the best I'd had in a long time. We talked about everything, from our childhoods to our favorite movies, and I felt so comfortable with him like I could be completely myself without any pretense.

Two days after that incredible birthday lunch, James and I went on our first official date. I was nervous, of course, but also incredibly excited. There was something about James that just felt right, something that told me this wasn't going to be like any other relationship I'd had before. And I was right. The connection between us was immediate and electric. It was unlike anything I'd ever experienced. We had so much in common, and our conversations flowed naturally, without any awkward silences or forced topics.

There's one moment from that date that I'll never forget. We were sitting close to each other, so close that I could feel the warmth of his body next to mine. He looked into my eyes with such intensity, like he could see right into my soul. Before he could say anything, I blurted out, "I now see it." He looked a bit puzzled and asked, "What do you mean?"

I took a deep breath and explained, "Have you ever heard the saying, 'When you meet the one, you'll realize why it never worked out with anyone else'?" For a moment, James just looked at me, and then he smiled—a smile that made my heart skip a beat. Without saying a word, he leaned in and kissed me, a kiss that was both tender and passionate. When he pulled back, he whispered, "That's exactly how I feel."

At that moment, everything made sense. All the heartbreaks, the failed relationships, and the lonely nights, they all led me to this point, to this person who made me feel more alive than I had ever felt before. It was like finding the missing piece of a puzzle I didn't even know I was putting together. With James, everything just clicked, and I knew that whatever happened next, we were meant to be in each other's lives.

James and I definitely didn't have what you'd call a typical relationship. From the very beginning, we bypassed the usual stages of getting to know each other and just dove straight into being together. It was exciting, intense, and a little overwhelming all at once. As time went on, the challenges we faced became more apparent. We were constantly dealing with obstacles that seemed to come from every direction, even internally from each other. The truth is, not only were there people around us who simply didn't want to see us happy or together and doing everything they could to drive a wedge between us, but James and I both had our own faults.

I'm not going to pretend that we were perfect, far from it. There were moments when I was angry, frustrated, and hurt by the way things unfolded between us. In spite of everything, when I first met James, I saw something in him that I couldn't ignore. I saw the good in him, the potential for greatness. He was an amazing man with so much love and kindness to offer, especially when it came to his family. James was a family man through and through, and he had a genuine love for children that I found incredibly endearing.

I remember vividly how James would look at me with a smile and say, "This time next year, we'll be strolling down the street with our daughter." It was a vision of the future that he held onto tightly, one that I wanted to believe in as well. He was already expecting his first child with another woman, and, at first, that was a tough pill to swallow. I couldn't quite wrap my head around how he could be having a child with someone he wasn't in love with. However, love is complicated, and so is life. Despite my initial hesitation, I loved him, and because of that love, I accepted the situation with open arms. We talked often about how we would raise his child together and how we'd eventually have a daughter of our own. It was a dream we both cherished, even if the reality was much more convoluted.

As our relationship progressed, I started to see cracks in the foundation. James didn't really know how to have a healthy relationship. He would lie to me about the smallest things, things that didn't even seem worth lying about. His dishonesty left me speechless and confused. I kept asking myself, "Why does he feel the need to lie?" It wasn't just the lies, though. James had a habit of disappearing on me, sometimes for days at a time. He would leave without a word, and I would be left in a state of constant worry, wondering if he was okay, if he was coming back, if we were still even together.

These disappearances gave me so much heartache. I started to question everything about our relationship and myself. I felt like I wasn't good enough for him like there was something inherently wrong with me that made him behave this way. I had never felt so insecure in my life as I did when I was with James. The doubts crept in, and they were relentless. I began to wonder if he was just using me if there was some ulterior motive behind his actions. I couldn't understand how a man like him, who loved the lavish life and all the finer things, could want to be with someone like me. I'm not ugly, but I've never considered myself the prettiest either. I'm just a simple woman who doesn't care much for extravagance. All I've ever wanted is to be loved and respected.

James, on the other hand, seemed to thrive in the world of luxury. He enjoyed the luxurious things in life, while I was content with the simple pleasures. This difference between us only added to my insecurities. I would look at him and wonder, "What does he see in me? Why is he with me when he could have anyone he wants?" It was a question that haunted me, and the lack of answers made it all the more painful.

Despite all the love I had for James, these uncertainties slowly began to eat away at me. I started to feel like I was losing myself in the relationship, that I was compromising who I was just to keep him happy. Unfortunately, even as these feelings grew stronger, I couldn't bring myself to walk away. There was something about James, something that kept me holding on, even when it hurt.

James' baby mama, whose name shall not be mentioned, had him wrapped around her finger in ways that I never imagined possible. I knew from the start that their situation was complicated, but I underestimated just how much control she had over him. For the sake of his unborn child, James was essentially her puppet, following her every demand without question. It was hard to watch, especially because she never knew about me, but I knew everything about her. Thanks to some late-night Google searches, I had pieced together a clear picture of who she was and the role she played in James' life.

This dynamic caused a lot of friction between James and me. The more he catered to her whims, the more distant we became. I could feel him slipping away, and there was nothing I could do to stop it. Nights that should have been filled with love and laughter were instead spent crying into my pillow, wondering how things had gone so wrong. I even found myself starving for days, not out of any conscious decision but because the pain in my heart had taken away my appetite. All I wanted was a simple, happy life with James, but it felt like that dream was slipping further out of reach with every passing day.

James is the type of man who hates drama, and he would go to great lengths to avoid it. But in trying to keep the peace with everyone else, he neglected the most important person in his life, me. Communication was our biggest downfall. He knew I was hurting, that I was constantly disappointed, but he never truly understood the depth of my love for him. I loved him wholeheartedly and was willing to work through any issue if it meant we could be happy together. But without open and honest communication, we were doomed to fail.

Two weeks before my birthday, something shifted between us. James and I decided to give our relationship another shot, and for a brief moment, it felt like we were back on track. The man I had fallen in love with was back—the caring, loving, and attentive James that made my heart race. We worked through our issues, and one thing I always appreciated about James was his ability to apologize when he knew he had messed up. It wasn't easy for him, but he did it because he cared. I admired him for that. But as much as he tried, there was still one major problem: James couldn't be fully honest with me.

The day before my birthday, James dropped a bombshell on me. He told me he had to leave town for a last-minute work emergency. My heart sank. A part of me shattered at that moment, and I tried to salvage what was left. I told him, "Okay, screw it! Let's go together, and I'll cancel my birthday party." I was willing to sacrifice my own plans just to be with him, but he reassured me that he would be back in time for the party. Deep down, I knew he wasn't coming back, and that this was probably the end of our relationship. But I held onto hope, even though every instinct told me otherwise.

As my birthday came and went, and James never showed up, I felt the last threads of trust I had in him snap. I was already trying to rebuild my faith in him, but this was the final blow. I couldn't understand why he couldn't just be honest with me, why he had to lie about something so important. I spent the night of my birthday asking myself over and over, "What did I do to deserve this? Why wasn't I good enough? Why couldn't James either love me correctly or just let me go completely?" The questions haunted me, for there were no answers.

Chapter: 20
Karma and Inner Strength

The truth is our relationship was toxic. We were both holding on, but in doing so, we were slowly destroying each other. Neither of us could fully let go, but staying together was causing us both so much pain. It was a vicious cycle of love, hurt, and disappointment, and it was taking its toll on me. I knew I had to find a way to move on, but the thought of living without James was almost too much to bear.

After about three months, I began to forget about James. The pain that once consumed me started to fade, and I found myself slowly moving on with my life. My wounds, though still tender, began to heal. It was a difficult process, but I knew I had to keep going. The funny thing is, James knew all about Henry and what he had done to me. He knew the pain I had endured, the betrayal I had felt. I thought that after everything, James would love me unconditionally, that he would see the hurt I had been through and cherish me even more. But I was wrong.

I can't lie, those first three months without James were some of the hardest I've ever faced. Mentally, I felt like I was spiraling into darkness. I completely isolated myself from the world, cutting off friends and family because I couldn't bear to let anyone see the state I was in. I lost so much weight that I barely recognized myself in the mirror. Food lost its taste, and the simplest tasks felt like insurmountable challenges. I didn't want to live anymore. The thought of continuing on without James was unbearable.

What hurt the most was trying to understand how he could have done this to me. I couldn't wrap my head around the fact that someone I loved so deeply, someone I would have given my life for, had played me like a fool. I kept replaying our moments together, trying to pinpoint where things went wrong, but the answers eluded me. It felt like a cruel joke, and I was the punchline.

In all honesty, I would have given everything for James. I would have stood by him through anything, but in the end, that loyalty wasn't enough. He broke me in ways I never thought possible, and it took every ounce of strength I had to start picking up the pieces of my shattered heart. Those three months were a battle, a test of my resilience, and though I came out the other side, the scars of what I went through will always remain.

I hadn't seen James for four months. We had blocked each other on everything imaginable, erasing our connection as thoroughly as we could. In spite of the distance and the silence, I couldn't shake him from my mind. During those months, I learned through friends—and a little social media sleuthing, that James had become a father, welcoming a beautiful, healthy baby boy into the world. No matter what had happened between us, one thing I knew for certain was that James was an amazing father. No one could convince me otherwise. Even though he had no idea, I kept tabs on him, quietly following the journey of him and his son from afar.

I saw the lavish party he threw to celebrate his son's arrival, a grand event filled with joy and extravagance. The photos from the party, shared by mutual friends, showed James beaming with pride, holding his son close. There were also family photos that included the mother of his child. They looked so perfect together, like a family out of a magazine. It was painful to see, but I tried to make sense of it. I told myself, "Maybe this is all God's plan. Maybe they are meant to be a happy family for the sake of their child." I clung to that thought, trying to find some solace in the idea that everything was happening for a reason.

I knew in my heart that James never truly loved her, not in the way he had claimed to love me. But after the birth of his son, I figured that maybe things had changed. Maybe the responsibility of parenthood had brought them closer, and they were trying to make it work for the sake of their child. I wanted to believe that he was happy, even if it wasn't with me.

Yet, not a single day went by when I didn't think of James. His memory lingered like a shadow, always present, always pulling at my heart. I constantly wondered what he was up to, if he was content with his life, and if he ever thought of me. The ache of missing him never dulled, and every time I allowed myself to dwell on it, I would break down crying. The tears came easily, as did the frustration with myself for still caring so deeply about someone who had hurt me so much.

I couldn't understand why I missed him so intensely. How could I still long for a man who had shattered my heart and destroyed the dreams we once shared? I had been ready to marry him, to build a life together, and nothing else mattered to me. I had even told him I would sign a prenup because I didn't care about his money or his possessions, I only wanted him. But that dream was gone, and I was left grappling with the reality of a love that had been one-sided, of a future that would never be.

Since our relationship ended, I have run into James a few times while driving around town. Each time, it felt like my heart stopped for a second, and a wave of tears would burst out uncontrollably. Seeing him stirred up a mix of emotions—sadness, anger, and a deep, burning hatred. I wanted him to be miserable. I craved revenge. I hated him so much that even hearing his name made my blood boil. I wished for nothing good to come his way, fueled by the overwhelming hatred that had taken root in my heart.

During our separation, I began uncovering the layers of lies he had buried me under. I found out that while I was faithfully committed to him, he had been cheating on me with multiple women. Those times when he would disappear for days, leaving me in a state of worry and confusion, he was actually with the mother of his child, taking care of her. But oddly enough, it wasn't the infidelity that crushed me the most. What truly killed me was finding out that he cheated on me with a woman who wasn't even close to being my equal. She was a nasty-looking gold digger, someone I knew all too well.

James always reassured me that there was nothing going on between them, and the woman herself played along, telling me the same thing. She would message me, acting like she was my friend, telling me how much James loved me and how excited he was to celebrate my birthday. She even went so far as to text me a picture of a Balmain purse, claiming that James had bought it for my birthday to surprise me. I was taken in by her charade, believing that she was genuinely on my side.

This woman was crafty, I'll give her that. She made sure to keep her competition close, pretending to be my friend while secretly stabbing me in the back. We even ended up working together, and she did everything she could to worm her way into my life. She knew I was head over heels for James, and it killed her. All she wanted was James for herself, and she made sure to destroy us. She slept with my man multiple times, and then had the audacity to smile in my face, asking if we were becoming good friends. She would buy me coffee, shower me with fake kindness, all while knowing she was betraying me.

Women like that are desperate and disgusting. They don't care about ruining someone else's happiness as long as they can claim a piece of it for themselves, even if it means being nothing more than a man's mistress for a short period of time. The betrayal cut deep, not just because of James, but because of the calculated cruelty of someone I had thought was a friend. The realization that I had been played by both of them filled me with a rage that I struggled to contain. I wanted them both to suffer the way I was suffering.

In those moments, all the love I had once felt for James was consumed by the hatred of how thoroughly they had both deceived me. It's a bitter pill to swallow, knowing that someone you loved could do something so cruel, and that someone you trusted could betray you in such a vile way. But as much as I wanted to see them both destroyed, I knew that letting that hatred fester would only continue to poison me. The path to healing was not going to be easy, and the scars of this betrayal would linger, but I knew I had to find a way to let go, for my own sake. I couldn't let them continue to have that power over me.

See, this isn't my first rodeo. Henry also had a friend who he claimed was like a sister to him. Let me tell you, this chick was something else. She had a way of making sure that whatever she said to Henry, he would believe it without question. It was her word against everyone else's, and Henry loved her so much that I had to question their relationship numerous times. He swore up and down that nothing had ever happened between them, that she was just like a sister to him, but I couldn't shake the feeling that there was something more, at least on her end. My gut told me she liked him more than a friend, even if Henry couldn't or wouldn't, see it.

She was always in the know, aware of all of Henry's secrets, and somehow, she always made sure that I found out about them too. She was sneaky, that's for sure. She tried hard to become great friends with my bestie Mina and me, constantly messaging to see what was going on in our group, what Henry was up to, and how our relationship was going. But I knew better than to open my mouth to her. She loved gossip and would pounce on any scrap of information to twist it for her own purposes. I could see right through her, but Mina, bless her heart, wasn't as careful. Mina thought that since this girl was so close to Henry, maybe she could talk some sense into him, especially when we were fighting. But that was a huge mistake.

Instead of helping, Henry's friend would twist every story, making things worse between Henry and me. She would go back to him with a completely skewed version of events, causing huge fights between us. It wasn't enough for her to just stir the pot; she would go so far as to try and undermine Henry to me directly. She'd say things like, "Henry's just playing games with you.

86

You deserve someone better." It was painfully obvious that she hated the idea of Henry and me being together. She didn't want us to be happy, didn't want us to work things out, and every time I was around, she'd barely show her face. Now that I'm out of Henry's life, she's suddenly there every day, always sitting right next to him.

It's laughable, really, because she claims to be close to Henry's wife, yet she's perfectly fine with Henry cheating on her. How can you call yourself someone's friend and then turn around and enable their husband to cheat? And then she has the nerve to smile in Henry's wife's face like nothing's wrong. It's beyond disgusting. People like that, people who are dirty and grimy, who thrive on creating drama and tearing others down, make me sick. They pretend to be your friend, but all they care about is their own agenda, no matter who they hurt along the way.

In this situation with James, it felt like history was repeating itself. I was once again dealing with someone who seemed determined to undermine me and my relationship. The difference this time was that I had grown stronger, wiser, and more protective of my self-respect. I wasn't going to let anyone walk all over me or drag me down into the muck of their drama.

Some people might have clapped back, igniting a firestorm of conflict and chaos, but I've learned that there's far more power in silence than in yelling and screaming. Silence, in many ways, speaks louder. It's a form of control, a way to rise above the pettiness and refuse to give others the reaction they crave.

I've always believed in karma, what goes around, comes around. It's a fundamental truth that keeps me grounded. That's why, instead of getting entangled in unnecessary battles, I choose to walk away. I choose to sit quietly, knowing that, eventually, life has a way of balancing the scales. My silence isn't a weakness; it's a strength. It's the knowledge that I don't need to prove anything to anyone or lower myself to their level. I trust that the universe will take care of the rest, and in the meantime, I'll continue to protect my peace and my dignity.

Going back to James, I truly thought I'd never hear from him again. I had tried a couple of times to reach out, hoping we could at least have a civil conversation, maybe find some closure so we could both move on. But after months of silence, I had pretty much given up. Then, one morning in late spring, something unexpected happened. I woke up around 6:30 am, groggy and still half-asleep, and checked my phone out of habit. To my surprise, I saw a notification: a text from James. I literally laughed out loud, thinking I was still dreaming because I'd had so many nights where I imagined having conversations with him in my sleep. It seemed surreal like one of those vivid dreams you're sure is real until you wake up fully.

So, I tossed my phone aside and decided to catch another 20 minutes of sleep, convincing myself that I could deal with whatever this was later. When I finally pulled myself out of bed, I opened the window blinds to let the morning light flood in and lit a candle, something I did to center myself at the start of each day. But there was this nagging thought in the back of my mind, pulling me back to that notification. I picked up my phone again, and there it was, glaring at me: James Z has sent you a text message. I couldn't stop staring at it, my heart pounding with a mix of anticipation and dread. What could he possibly want after all this time? Why now?

I hesitated, my thumb hovering over the notification, afraid to open it because I didn't know what to expect. I didn't know how to feel or what he even wanted after all these months. My mind raced with possibilities, each one more nerve-wracking than the last. So, I waited about 30 minutes, just trying to gather my thoughts to prepare myself for whatever was coming. I couldn't help but feel that his message was going to reopen old wounds, stir up emotions I'd tried so hard to bury, and maybe even lead to another heated argument.

Finally, I took a deep breath and opened the text. And all I saw was, "HI, Sammy." My first reaction? Annoyance. "HI Sammy"? First off, it's "Sami," not "Sammy." How could he spell my name wrong after everything? It felt like a slap in the face like he didn't even care enough to get that right. It was such a small thing, but it hit a nerve. My irritation flared up, and I decided I wasn't going to let him off easy. So, I replied with a bit of an attitude: "What do you want?"

He quickly responded, asking me to call him because he needed to talk to me about something.

The way he phrased it made my stomach drop. I knew that tone; it meant something had happened, and it probably wasn't good. I could feel an argument brewing already, just from those few words. I took a moment to steady myself, running through all the things I wanted to say, all the pent-up frustration and hurt I'd been carrying. I was ready to unleash it all, ready for whatever confrontation was about to come.

I called him, my voice cool and guarded, and asked why he was reaching out so early in the morning. But as soon as he spoke, something in his voice caught my attention. He sounded sad, almost broken, and that threw me off balance. I didn't want him to know how much I had missed him, how those four months had been a brutal battle with myself just to keep from spiraling back into the darkness, how I had to start from scratch to rebuild the life he had destroyed, or how hard it had been to piece together the fragments of my shattered heart.

James said he wanted to have a sit-down conversation to finally see things through. He acknowledged that I had every right to hang up, to walk away and leave this chapter behind, but something in his words, in the way he said it, made it impossible for me to just hang up. Despite everything, I wasn't that type of person. So, I told him that if he was ready to be completely honest and tell the truth about everything that had happened, then I would be open to meeting.

He sounded relieved, almost happy that I was willing to talk, and before I knew it, I found myself getting ready to meet him. An hour later, I was pulling up to his place. My heart pounded in my chest, a chaotic mix of fear and anticipation. I had no idea how I would feel seeing him again or how he would react to seeing me. The fear that all the old feelings, both love and anger, would come rushing back was almost paralyzing. But there I was, standing in front of his door, the point of no return.

For a moment, I considered turning around, pretending something had come up, or just running away altogether. But I knew he had seen me pull up. There was no escaping this now. I took a deep breath and gave a soft knock on the door, barely even touching it before it swung open. And there he was, James, standing right in front of me, looking like a ghost from my past.

Every instinct screamed at me to jump into his arms, to hold him tight, but I forced myself to stay cool, to keep my emotions in check. I couldn't even bring myself to look him in the eyes.

Instead, I stood there awkwardly, my hand halfway extended as if to offer a handshake. A handshake, seriously? How do you even greet your ex in a situation like this? Is there some kind of protocol for these things? I felt ridiculous standing there like that, but I didn't know what else to do.

He didn't reach out for the handshake. Instead, he just stood there for a moment, looking at me like he was seeing a ghost too. Finally, he stepped aside to let me in, and as I walked past him into the house, I could feel the tension thick in the air. Neither of us knew what to say or how to act. It was like stepping onto a minefield; one wrong move could cause everything to explode.

I sat on the couch, barely able to look at him. No matter what he was saying or asking, I kept my eyes glued to the floor, to my hands, anywhere but his face. I knew that if I met his gaze, the feelings I had worked so hard to bury would come rushing back, and I couldn't afford that. We sat on separate couches, a chasm of space between us filled with all the things we hadn't said. It felt strange, surreal even, to be sitting in his home, the home he shared with the mother of his child.

I couldn't help but let my eyes wander around the room, taking in the details of the life he had built without me. I listened intently, half-expecting to hear the soft cry of a baby from another room. I was desperate to catch a glimpse of his son, wondering what he looked like, what he smelled like, and how it would feel to hold him close, to kiss his tiny cheeks. I imagined what it would have been like if things had been different if James and I had stayed together, if I had been part of this little family.

But the house was quiet, too quiet. There was no sign of a baby, no sounds of life beyond the two of us. The silence was heavy, almost suffocating. I finally managed to break it, congratulating him on becoming a father. Instead of the warm smile I expected, his face fell. He muttered something under his breath, so low I almost didn't catch it: "I have to talk to you about that."

My stomach tightened into knots. What could he possibly have to say that would make him look so somber? My mind raced through all the possibilities, each one more terrifying than the last.

What could have happened? Was something wrong with his son? Did it somehow involve me? The tension was unbearable, but before I could ask him to elaborate, he got up and suggested we go downstairs to check on his neighbor's daughter. I didn't know what else to do, so I followed him.

We found his neighbor's daughter playing outside, and James invited her back up to his place to spend some time with me. I tried to focus on the little girl, on her innocent laughter and the way she looked up at me with wide, curious eyes. But all I could think about was the unfinished conversation, the bombshell James seemed ready to drop at any moment. The more I tried to push it away, the more it consumed me. I knew we would eventually confront whatever it was he had to say. In the meantime, we were sitting there, making small talk with a child between us, pretending like everything was fine, even though the tension was thick enough to cut with a knife.

As we moved into the baby's room, I felt an overwhelming sense of unease. The room was a mess, as if it had been hastily abandoned. There was no sign of a baby ever having slept there, no toys or blankets, just a cold, empty space. My mind raced with possibilities, each one darker than the last. Where was the baby? Was he okay? I had never met James' child, yet I found myself filled with concern for his well-being, as if he were my own. It was irrational, maybe even foolish, but I couldn't help it. This child, who I had only known through stories and photos, had somehow found a place in my heart.

As we sat down, I noticed James' eyes were glassy, on the brink of tears. I could see he was holding back, trying to maintain control. I wanted so badly to comfort him, to tell him that everything would be okay, that he could confide in me. Maybe, just maybe, he would finally be honest with me. I still kept my distance, unsure of what was coming, and wary of offering forgiveness too soon. My heart was pounding, my mind racing with anticipation and fear. James took a deep breath, and when he finally spoke, his words shattered the silence. "She took my son left to another state without me knowing."

The impact of those words hit me like a punch to the gut. I could feel the tears welling up in my eyes, but I blinked them back, determined not to let them fall. I knew how much his son meant to him. James had always talked about his son as if he were the center of his universe, the one thing he would sacrifice everything for. To hear that his son had been taken away was more than I could bear.

Anger surged through me, not at James, but at his baby mama. How could she do this? How could she take his child and leave without a word? It was cruel, heartless. My mind was filled with images of her, someone I had never met but now hated with every fiber of my being. James wasn't a deadbeat dad. He had done everything for her, provided her with a beautiful apartment, a nice car, anything she needed to focus on their son. He had given her everything, more than he had ever given me, and for what? To be betrayed like this?

Chapter: 21
Show Don't Tell

I felt a pang of jealousy mixed with the hurt. Why had he been so willing to go above and beyond for someone he didn't even love, while I was left to fend for myself during my darkest times? Why did he always run to her aid and not mine when I was at my lowest? It didn't make sense. I knew James had a temper, which had always been his downfall. Crazy James, the side of him that I had only heard about, was terrifying to others, but he had never shown it to me. He had never laid a hand on me, never raised his voice in a way that made me feel threatened. That was one of the things I had loved most about him—his ability to control his anger, to walk away rather than hurt me. He'd gotten into a fight with his baby mama about something—God knows what—and she decided to take their son and leave him, moving to a different state without his knowledge. Watching him go through that, I started to wonder if he really loved her, at least as the mother of his child. After all, he had written a book for his son and even mentioned her in it.

But now, seeing him on the verge of breaking down, I realized just how much he had been holding in. I knew he was struggling, torn apart by the loss of his son, and I wanted nothing more than to help him. Nevertheless, I also knew that I had to protect myself. I couldn't afford to get sucked back into the chaos, into the web of lies and half-truths that had defined our relationship. So, I sat there, in the room that should have been filled with the sounds of a baby, and listened as James poured out his heart. I listened, and I waited, hoping that this time, he would be completely honest with me, that we could finally have the conversation we had both been avoiding for so long.

James knew my history of abuse, and he understood that if he ever crossed the line by verbally or physically abusing me, it would have pushed me into a very dark place. He was fully aware that any form of abuse would make me fear him, and that's not what he wanted. I know that James loved me, even though he was often terrible at showing it. His main fear was disappointing me. He couldn't stand the thought of seeing me frown at him or feeling like he had let me down. But that was never my intention. All I ever wanted was to build a beautiful life together, to create something lasting and meaningful with him.

James was incredibly smart, probably one of the smartest people I've ever known. He had a natural talent for hustling, for taking nothing and turning it into something valuable. That was one of the things I admired most about him. James didn't have an easy start in life; he came from nothing and had a past filled with challenges. He had gotten into trouble growing up, but that didn't stop him from working hard to build a better life and take care of his family.

When James opened his first business, he was unstoppable. He was making more money in six months than most people could make in a year. It takes time to build a comfortable life, usually a year or more, but James did it in record time. He worked every holiday, pulled countless all-nighters, all to ensure that his family was always taken care of. His dedication paid off when he was able to move his entire family into a beautiful home up in the mountains. I knew how much making his family proud, especially his mother, meant to him, and he did that—he made them proud.

I never told James just how proud I was of him. I kept those feelings to myself, partly because I didn't want to inflate his ego. I didn't want him to think that he had reached the pinnacle of success because, in my eyes, he hadn't. I wanted him to keep pushing, to continue hustling, to aim even higher in life. I saw so much potential in him, and I wanted him to do more, to achieve bigger things, not just for himself, but for the empire we could have built together.

Sitting with him, I thought about all I knew about James and what I had loved about him, I mustered the courage to ask him what had happened, and if he knew why she decided to just get up and leave. She was so loved by his family; they did everything for her. Whatever she wanted, he would give it to her without hesitation. I mean, she received two Chanel bags just for being pregnant, and a Hermès stroller and blanket for the baby. While I'm not one to care about materialistic things, it still stung to see how he prioritized her over everyone else, including me. I always felt like I was on the back burner in his life, never truly a priority. It was like I was only important when times were tough or when he was lonely. Only then would he reach out to me.

I could never wrap my head around why he even wanted to be with me if he wasn't serious about us. No matter how many times we broke up, no matter how many days we went without speaking, we would always find a way back to each other. It was a cycle I despised. I hated being that girl—the one who forgives so easily, who lets people back into her life no matter how much pain they've caused. James was my weakness, and deep down, I knew he still was. I kept telling myself that maybe, just maybe, I could change him, help him become the man I believed he could be. But I was wrong. I couldn't change him. James needs to change for himself, to be a better man for himself, and for any woman he might be with in the future.

When James reached out to me, I allowed myself to hope that maybe, just maybe, things would finally be different. I thought that perhaps he had changed, that he was ready to work things out and build something real with me. But as I sit here now, I realize how wrong I was—or at least, that's how I'm feeling at this moment. When I went over to his house, I saw a man who was hurting deeply, and despite everything he'd done to me, I couldn't find it in my heart to kick him while he was down. That's not who I am. This man, who I once saw as invincible, was now broken. He cried for days, fell into a deep depression, and completely shut down. He stopped eating, stopped showering, and wouldn't even leave his house. The only thing he wanted to do was drink—starting from the moment he woke up until he could finally pass out again. I wanted to be there for him, to be his support system, to help him get through the pain he was experiencing.

I couldn't stand seeing him like that. I wanted to bring back the James I knew, the fun-loving guy who always wanted to have a good time, who could light up a room with his smile. But it felt impossible because he's so damn hard-headed. He never wanted to listen to anyone, and he always thought he was right about everything. With James, it was his way or the highway, and there was never any room for compromise.

One thing I learned from being with James is that when he truly loves someone, when he loves them with his whole heart, he goes above and beyond for them. He pours everything he has into that person. As we talked, I couldn't shake the feeling of how much I wished he had given me precedence in his life like he did with others. I wanted to be the one he would go above and beyond for, instead, I was the one who was always there when he needed something, never truly feeling like I was valued for who I was. I realized that loving James meant accepting the fact that I could never change him; he had to want that change for himself. I always felt like I was chasing something I could never fully have. I was chasing the idea of him, the potential I saw, rather than the reality of who he was. That's a hard truth to accept, and that's when it hit me: no matter how much I loved him, it was time to let go of the hope that I could fix things or that he would suddenly become the man I needed him to be. It was time to accept that some people come into our lives to teach us lessons, and that love doesn't always mean holding on, it sometimes means letting go.

When I met James, he had a saying that I truly believed he lived by: "I trust and respect you until you give me a reason not to." He always said that trust and respect didn't need to be earned, they were given freely, and it was up to the other person to maintain them. You would think someone with that kind of mindset would actually take their own advice, but James didn't. He lied to me, broke me, and for what? Did he think he loved me, or was it just because I was an Afghan woman, someone who would make his family happy? I don't think he will ever truly love me the way I deserve to be loved, not in the deep, meaningful way that I crave.

And that realization hurts more than anything. I've spent so much time and energy on James, hoping that he would change, that he would finally see me for who I am and love me as I deserve to be loved. But deep down, I know that he's not capable of giving me that. He's too wrapped up in his own world, in his own pain and insecurities, to ever truly be there for me. And as much as I want to be there for him, as much as I want to help him through his struggles, I can't keep sacrificing my own happiness and well-being for someone who doesn't see my worth.

It's time for me to let go of the hope that things will change, to accept that James is who he is, and that he's not the man I need him to be. It's time for me to move on and find someone who will love me the way I deserve to be loved, without lies, without games, and without the constant pain. I deserve better, and it's time I started believing that.

After I saw James and learned what happened to his son, I felt an overwhelming urge to be there for him. I tried to check in on him as much as I could, hoping to offer some comfort during what I knew was an incredibly difficult time for him. But James remained the same, distant, unresponsive, and emotionally unavailable. It felt like I had been burned all over again, and I couldn't help but feel foolish and stupid for even trying to be there for him. I had a gut feeling that maybe his baby mama and son had returned and that James was happy again, no longer needing me. That realization stung deeply. Even though I felt all the old pain rushing back, I knew that this time, I was stronger. I refused to let him break me completely again, but it still hurt because I had allowed him back into my life, knowing full well the risks involved.

For a week, I couldn't sleep. I worried constantly about him, wondering if he had eaten, if he was sleeping, what he was doing, or who he was with. I kept asking myself, "Why? Why am I allowing him to consume my days and cause me sleepless nights again?" Seeing James, a man who was always so strong and unaffected by anything, in such a hopeless state, in tears, touched my heart me in a way I hadn't expected. I can never forget the moment I saw him break down. After my visit ended, I sat in my car and cried my eyes out because I felt so sorry for him. I wanted him to be with his son more than anything in the world. I wanted him to be happy, and I wanted to be there for him in any way I could.

But deep down, I knew that it wasn't my fault he was in pain, and it wasn't my responsibility to make him feel better. I felt like I had committed a sin because of all the horrible things we did to each other when we stopped talking. I had wished nothing good for him and prayed that he would get what was coming to him for what he did to me. I had wanted more than anything for him to feel the pain I had felt. As time went on, I realized that my wish for karma to strike him was only poisoning me. I had to snap out of it and remind myself that what he was going through had nothing to do with me.

The story between James and me is completely finished. I've closed that chapter in my life because I've come to understand that he was never going to change, and I deserve better than someone who couldn't be honest or emotionally present. I don't want someone who could physically or emotionally harm others in my life, and I'm finally at peace with that decision.

As for Henry, I know that story is still unfinished, but I'm okay with that. We're rebuilding a friendship, focusing on creating a healthier, more trustworthy relationship. We see each other all the time, and I'm content with where we are now. It's a different path, one that might not have a romantic ending, but it's a path I'm willing to explore, knowing that it's built on truth and mutual respect.

Chapter: 22
Reflecting on James

When I reflect on James and our time together, I do not always regret what we once had. I'm trying to understand him, our relationship, and what happened between us so that I can learn from the situation so and never repeat any mistakes. When I was with James, he had a way of always wanting me by his side, no matter what he was doing. At one point in our relationship, he mentioned that he wanted to take me out on a date, but before that, he needed to stop by his partner's house so I could meet him. He didn't provide much detail, just casually mentioned it in passing, so I didn't think much of it. But as we pulled up to this massive, imposing estate, I immediately felt like I had stepped into a scene straight out of a mafia movie.

The first thing that struck me was the sheer number of guards stationed everywhere. They weren't just standing around either, they were fully alert, scanning the area with intense, watchful eyes. It was as if we had driven into a high-security fortress rather than someone's home. The property itself was sprawling, with manicured lawns stretching as far as I could see and what seemed like a small army of security personnel at every turn. The entire atmosphere was both intimidating and surreal.

As we got closer to the house, my jaw nearly dropped at the sight before me. It wasn't just a home; it was a car museum. The number of exotic cars parked in front of the house was mind-blowing. Ferraris, Lamborghinis, Bugattis, you name it, it was there. The gleaming, polished exteriors of these high-end vehicles reflected the bright lights, making the entire scene look like something out of a dream. I couldn't help but be awestruck by the sheer display of wealth and power.

Before we entered the house, I realized I really needed to use the restroom, so I mentioned it to James. He nodded and immediately called over one of the guards, instructing him to escort me to the private bathroom in the guardhouse. The guard led me through a maze of pathways, past even more security checkpoints, until we reached a small, discreet building that looked more like a high-tech control center than a restroom facility.

Stepping inside, I was greeted by walls lined with monitors displaying live camera feeds from all over the property. It was like something out of a James Bond movie, cameras everywhere, capturing every angle, every movement. The entire setup was designed for maximum security, with state-of-the-art technology that felt both futuristic and slightly unnerving. Even the bathroom itself was sleek and modern, almost sterile in its precision.

As I washed my hands, I couldn't help but feel like I was part of something much bigger than I had ever imagined. The whole experience felt surreal, like I was living in a different world, one where luxury and danger coexisted in a delicate balance. When I finally rejoined James, I couldn't shake the feeling that I had just been given a glimpse into a life that was far removed from my own, a life of unimaginable wealth, power, and secrecy. It was an experience I would never forget, one that left me both fascinated and slightly uneasy.

When I walked into the house, I was immediately overwhelmed by its size and opulence. The sheer scale of the place was disorienting, and before I knew it, I was lost. The hallways seemed to stretch endlessly, lined with expensive artwork and decor that screamed wealth and power. My heart started to race as I realized I had no idea where I was or how to find James. I began calling out his name, hoping he would hear me and come to my rescue, but the only response was the eerie silence of the massive, empty corridors.

My anxiety grew with every step I took. I was terrified of accidentally breaking something or even just looking too closely at anything, knowing I was surrounded by things that were probably worth more than I could ever imagine. Just as I was beginning to panic, I finally heard distant voices. I followed the sound down the long hallway and, to my surprise, found James sitting at a large table with a group of people. The atmosphere was tense and serious, and it quickly dawned on me that I had just walked into the middle of an important meeting.

James looked up and saw me standing there, clearly out of place. He quickly motioned for me to join them, introducing me to everyone at the table. I was completely taken aback. We hadn't discussed anything about me being part of this meeting or even being involved in his work. To my shock, James began speaking highly of me, telling everyone that he wanted me to join the team and work for them. My mind was racing; I had no idea this was coming, and I definitely didn't want to mix our personal relationship with business. In my experience, that never ends well.

I felt ambushed and cornered. It was clear James knew exactly what he was doing; he had strategically put me in a position where I couldn't easily refuse the offer without looking ungrateful or uncooperative in front of all these people. So, despite my reservations, I felt pressured to accept the offer. We spent the rest of the meeting going over my job description, and I tried to focus, but my mind was spinning with a mix of emotions, anger, confusion, and frustration.

As soon as we got into James' car after the meeting, I confronted him. I told him how much I disliked the way he had backed me into a corner without giving me any prior warning or even asking if this was something I wanted to do. I appreciated that he wanted me to be involved in his work and make more money, but I didn't want to be in a situation where my boyfriend was also my boss. It felt like a recipe for disaster.

James, always smooth and persuasive, explained that his intentions were pure. He told me he wanted us to build an empire together, to make more money so we could enjoy life, and, most importantly, to spend more time together since his work kept him so busy. His reasoning made sense, and I couldn't argue with the idea of spending more time with him. Reluctantly, I agreed but made it clear that I didn't appreciate being ambushed and that it shouldn't happen again.

A week later, I officially started my new job. My role was essentially to clean up the mess left by their previous employee, who had mismanaged client relations. I took on the responsibility of calling clients, posing as the manager of customer service, and working to smooth things over.

To my surprise, I found myself excelling in the role. I was good at it, really good. Within a few weeks, I had not only met but exceeded their expectations. James was proud of me, and even his partner, who had been skeptical at first, was impressed. It felt good to be recognized for my hard work, but there was still a part of me that worried about the implications of mixing business with our relationship. For now, though, things seemed to be going well, and I hoped that we could continue to balance our personal and professional lives without any major issues.

That evening, I had planned what I thought would be a perfect staycation, a little getaway where James and I could escape the chaos of our lives and just focus on each other. I booked a nice room, imagining a weekend of relaxation, good food, and uninterrupted time together.

James had been enthusiastic about the plan and said he'd join me after handling some work. It was supposed to be our time, a chance to reconnect and enjoy each other's company without any distractions.

As the evening rolled on, I checked into the hotel and sent James a text to let him know I was waiting for him. He replied that he had a work emergency but promised he would be there as soon as he was done. I settled in, trying to be patient, but as the hours passed with no word from him, my worry began to grow. I tried to reach him again and again, but every call went unanswered. My worry turned into anxiety, and by the time it was close to midnight, I was frantic.

I started reaching out to everyone I could think of, friends, colleagues, anyone who might know where James was. But no one knew anything. It felt like he had just vanished, and with each passing minute, my mind conjured up darker and darker scenarios. I was alone in a hotel room, desperate for any news, and the silence from James was suffocating.

Finally, I decided to call his partner. I was hesitant, I didn't want to cause any trouble for James or make it seem like I didn't trust him. But it was almost one in the morning, and I was out of options. When his partner answered the phone, I could barely hold back my tears. I tried to explain the situation without giving too much away, but my emotions got the better of me. His partner asked what was going on, and I broke down, telling him that I hadn't heard from James in hours and that I was scared something had happened.

His partner was calm and reassuring, but what he said next caught me completely off guard. He told me that there was no emergency, no situation that would keep James away. He said that James had been lying to me. I was stunned. I didn't want to believe it, but the evidence was piling up. I told his partner about the photo James had sent me earlier, a disturbing image of a man with his face cut in half, supposedly threatening James. His partner sighed and told me that the photo was fake, that no one was threatening them, and that James had made the whole thing Up. I was floored. How could this be happening? How could James lie about something so serious? I felt betrayed and confused, but I still didn't want to believe it. His partner asked me why I cared so much about James, and I realized he didn't know the full story. When I told him that James and I were in a relationship, his partner was silent for a moment, clearly taken aback. Then he dropped another bombshell:

he had no idea that James and I were together. He thought we were just friends.

The reality of the situation hit me like a ton of bricks. James had been lying to me, to his partner, to everyone. His partner then told me something that shattered whatever was left of my trust in James, he said that James was living with his baby mama and that they were still together. I felt my heart break all over again. Here I was, sitting alone in a hotel room, waiting for a man who was living a double life.

I started to cry, feeling utterly humiliated and betrayed. I told his partner how I was stuck at this hotel for the weekend, that James had left me there alone, and how I didn't know what to do. His partner was sympathetic and tried to comfort me, but his words only added to my confusion and hurt. He said that if he had known about our relationship, he would have never agreed to have us all work together. He even told me that I deserved better and that I should leave James.

At that moment, I knew he was right. Every instinct was telling me to walk away, to save myself from further pain, but I couldn't bring myself to do it. I was too wrapped up in the hope that there was some explanation, some way to salvage our relationship. Hours passed, and it was 4 a.m. before his partner called me back, saying he had spoken to James and that everything was fine. He told me James would call me when he woke up to explain everything.

But by then, my anger had taken over. How could everything be "fine" when my world felt like it was crumbling? His partner's advice to leave James echoed in my mind, but I didn't listen.

Instead, I stayed, waiting for James's call, clinging to the hope that he could somehow explain away all the lies and betrayals.

Looking back, I realize how deeply I was in denial, how much I wanted to believe in the fantasy James had created rather than face the painful reality. But in that moment, I was just a woman sitting alone in a hotel room, desperately hoping for a happy ending that was never going to come.

The next morning, as I packed my things to leave the hotel, I noticed James' bag sitting in the corner of the room. He had left it with me the night before, intending to pick it up later. Given everything that had happened, I found myself staring at that bag, filled with a mix of curiosity and dread. Normally, I would never go through someone else's belongings, but this time was different. After everything I had just learned, I needed to know the truth.

With trembling hands, I unzipped the bag. What I found inside confirmed all my worst suspicions. There were hotel receipts from various places, dates that lined up with times he claimed to be "working late" or on "business trips." And then, there they were, condoms. My heart sank. Any lingering doubt I had was erased at that moment. James had been living a double life, lying to me, and using me while continuing his other relationships. The man I thought I knew, the man I loved, was a complete stranger.

Just as I was processing the shock, my phone buzzed. It was a text from James. He asked how and where I was doing, as if nothing had happened, as if the night before had been perfectly normal. The audacity of it all made my blood boil. I couldn't hold back my anger any longer, I lashed out, sending him a string of furious messages. I called him out on all his lies, on the deceit, and on the way he had made me feel so small and insignificant.

But instead of apologizing, instead of even acknowledging what he had done, James turned it around on me. He accused me of overstepping by getting his partner involved, saying I had no right to do that. He was more concerned with the fact that his lies had been exposed than with the pain he had caused me. I told him that he had no right to put me in a position where I genuinely feared for his life, where I felt like I had no choice but to involve others because I thought he was in danger.

His response was cold and dismissive. He told me to leave his bag with the receptionist and that he would pick it up later. Then, he said something that cut deeper than anything else: he didn't want to talk to me ever again. Just like that, he was done with me, like I was disposable.

But I wasn't ready to let it end that way. I refused to leave the bag with the receptionist because I needed to see him face to face. I needed answers. I needed to understand why he had done this to me, why he had manipulated me, lied to me, and made me feel like I was going crazy. I wanted to confront him, to look him in the eyes and demand an explanation. I knew it wouldn't change anything, that it wouldn't take away the pain, but I needed that closure, even if it was just for my own peace of mind.

As I waited for my Uber in the hotel lobby, I was trying to focus on the work tasks James had assigned me, but I couldn't shake the unease that had settled in my gut. I found a secluded corner where I hoped no one would notice me. I just needed to get out of there without running into James. My heart raced when I suddenly heard his voice nearby. Panic gripped me, and I instinctively hid, praying he wouldn't spot me.

Then, my phone buzzed. It was James, calling and texting, his messages laced with fury. He demanded to know where I was, cussing me out for leaving. I quickly texted him back, lying that I had already left. His response was explosive. I could hear the rage in his voice through the phone, and I was terrified. James had never scared me like this before, and I didn't know what he might do if he found me.

When my Uber finally arrived, I bolted for the car as if my life depended on it. The relief I felt once I was safely inside the vehicle, it was overwhelming, but the fear still lingered. For about a month, I didn't see or hear from James. Even though we worked together, he wasn't coming into the office, and I requested to work from home as much as possible to avoid any chance of running into him.

One day, I decided it was time to end this chapter for good. I texted James, letting him know I was going to leave his bag at his doorstep and that I wanted to quit my job. It pained me that I had to leave a job I was good at, all because James couldn't keep his personal and professional life separate. He was sloppy, deceitful, and I realized that some things about him would never change.

I was so nervous about going to his house that I called Henry for support. I explained the situation, telling him everything that had been happening. I asked Henry to call me in 15 minutes if he didn't hear from me because I was genuinely scared of what James might do. I knew he was capable of a lot, and the last thing I wanted was a confrontation.

When I arrived at James' place, I dropped the bag off as quickly as I could and sprinted back to my car. My heart pounded the entire time. As soon as I was safely inside, I called Henry, telling him I was okay and that I was on my way to see him. I needed to be with Henry, my safe place, where I knew no one could harm me. The moment I saw Henry's face, the fear and anxiety melted away. My heart finally stopped racing, and I felt, if only for a moment, that everything was going to be alright.

Weeks went by, and I barely thought about James. I had begun to move on, focusing on my life without him. But just when I thought I was over him, James reappeared, like he always did, with perfect timing. He called me out of the blue, asking how I was and apologizing for everything.

He begged me to come back to work, promising that if we didn't get back together, it would be fine, but he desperately needed his business partner back. He claimed that without me, they were struggling to manage.

I agreed to return under strict conditions: I would work from home, and our communication would be minimal. He accepted these terms, but soon after, he insisted I come to the office for a meeting.

I should have known better, but I went, hoping it was just a routine work discussion.

Instead, I walked into an ambush. James, in front of everyone, announced that I was his girlfriend and that he loved me. He demanded that his colleagues and partners treat me with respect, or they would be fired.

It was all part of James' manipulative tactics to win me back, and once again, I fell for it. I found myself back in the same toxic cycle, unable to break free. I continued being with him, hoping things might be different this time, but deep down, I knew better. The truth of James' character was undeniable, and soon, my birthday came around, a day that would prove once again that James was incapable of change.

Chapter: 23
The Reason Why Love Hurts

It took me years to realize that the comfort I found in these toxic relationships was a reflection of my upbringing: my entire childhood was filled with toxicity. Growing up, I was surrounded by chaos, and it shaped the way I view love and relationships. I never had a healthy relationship with my family, especially not with my dad. The fear I had of him was overwhelming, and to be honest, I think I feared him more than God. I know that's a crazy thing to say, but when you're living in a poisonous household where physical abuse is the answer to everything, fear becomes your constant companion.

My dad had a serious drinking problem. Every day around 4 pm, like clockwork, a bottle of tequila would appear at home. That time of day wasn't for casual cocktails or a moment of relaxation; it was for shot after shot of numbing the pain he never talked about. I always asked him why he drank so much, and he would always say it helped him sleep. But for me, 4 pm became the most dreaded time of day because I knew that by 4:30 or 5 pm, all hell would break loose. My dad would snap at the smallest things, and no matter what I did, it was never good enough.

I was the daughter he never wanted. True story: when my mom was pregnant, the doctor made a mistake and told my parents I was going to be a boy. Imagine the surprise on the day I was born when the doctor said, "Congratulations! You have a daughter." My dad's reaction? He broke the video camera in the hospital and started a huge fight, declaring that he didn't want me. Imagine that—being born into a world where your own father didn't want you. How was it my fault that I was born a girl? I didn't ask to be alive; I didn't ask to be part of this family. But God had a plan, and I believe He knew my mom needed me.

I've always felt like my father didn't love me, and I've spent my life trying to understand why he was always so hard on me. He never told me he loved me, not once. Instead, he would put me down and compare me to others. For instance, he would tell me that I needed a nose job and that no man would ever want to be with me because I wasn't pretty. He barely ever hugged or kissed me. The affection I craved from him was always just out of reach. He would say things like, "Why can't you be like your cousins? Look at them and how amazing they are." Every time we would visit his sister's house, he would shower his niece with the love and attention I longed for. I was jealous of their bond, jealous of the amount of love my dad gave her. I always felt like I was in some kind of competition with her.

Because of this, my relationship with my cousin was complicated, to say the least. It was a lot of love and hate. On the one hand, I looked up to her like an older sister; on the other, I resented her for being everything my father wanted me to be. She was the straight-A student, the popular girl at school, the perfect child that every parent dreams of. She never seemed to get in trouble, and it was rare for anyone to raise their voice at her. She was my role model, and I tried to be like her in every way, hoping that maybe, just maybe, my father would start to appreciate and love me.

I spent my childhood and teenage years seeking my dad's approval, thinking that if I was good at something or achieved something amazing, he would finally tell me he was proud of me, that he loved me. I would see other fathers spoiling their daughters, loving them unconditionally, and I would pray every night for that kind of relationship with my dad. But it never came. Instead, I grew up feeling unworthy of love, constantly chasing validation from men who were just as toxic as the environment I grew up in.

Love hurts because I've never known a love that didn't. It was a strange kind of twisted love I felt, one that was deeply ingrained in me from years of being surrounded by turmoil. When you grow up in an environment where chaos is the norm, it becomes part of your identity. My father's rejection and the noxious dynamics in my family set the stage for a lifetime of seeking out relationships that mirror that pain. I've allowed men to treat me poorly because, deep down, it's the only kind of love I've ever known. As I reflect on all of this, I realize that I deserve more, I deserve a love that is kind, supportive, and unconditional. And while it's been a painful journey, I'm finally starting to understand that the love I've been searching for all along needs to start with loving myself.

My parents' financial struggles weren't just about money; they were about survival, about clinging to whatever we could in a world that often seemed to be collapsing around us. Their struggles seemed to seem into their relationship and ravaged any love or care they once had for each other. I remember the constant fights, the virulent words exchanged between them, and the way they looked at each other with pure disdain. They tried to get divorced so many times, but it was like a sick game—neither of them ever really followed through. Maybe it was because they were both afraid of what life would be like alone. Or maybe they were just too tired to finish what they started.

The venomous atmosphere in my home was suffocating. It wasn't just the screaming or the drunken nights; it was the silence that followed, the cold war that would last for days when no one spoke, and the tension was so thick you could feel it in the air, smothering you. I remember lying in bed, staring at the ceiling, wishing I could disappear. I didn't want to live there, didn't want to be a part of that never-ending cycle of anger and resentment. Unfortunately, every time I tried to leave, my mom would stop me. She'd cry and tell me that she couldn't survive without me, that if I left, she'd have nothing left to live for. And as much as I wanted to escape, I couldn't bear the thought of leaving her alone in that hell. So, I stayed, trapped by guilt and love and a sense of duty that I didn't fully understand.

The loneliness was the worst part. I had no friends, no one to talk to outside of my parents. I wasn't allowed to have a social life, and even if I could, I wouldn't have known how to start. My world was so small, confined to the walls of our home and the misery that lived there. I was a prisoner in my own life, and the worst part was, I didn't even realize it. I thought that was just how life was, that everyone lived like this.

Looking back now, it's no wonder I gravitated towards toxic men. It was all I knew. Healthy relationships were foreign to me; they felt unnatural, uncomfortable even. When someone treated me with kindness, I didn't know how to react. I distrusted it, waiting for the other shoe to drop, for the mask to slip to reveal their true self full of cruelty underneath. But if a man was cold, distant, or controlling, that felt familiar. It felt like home. I understood how to navigate a relationship where I had to fight for every scrap of affection, where love was conditional and could be taken away at any moment. It mirrored the dynamics I had grown up with, and even though it hurt, it was a pain I knew how to deal with.

I had been conditioned to believe that love was something you had to earn through suffering, that it was normal to be treated poorly as long as there were a few scraps of tenderness in between.

It's a hard habit to break, that belief that you're only as good as what someone else thinks of you, clinging to those relationships because they validated the pain I felt and reinforced the anger, sadness and feelings of worthlessness ingrained in me since childhood. I'm slowly learning that I deserve more than that and that I don't need to live like that anymore. I believe that I can have something better, that love shouldn't hurt, that the chaos I grew up in doesn't have to define the rest of my life, and that I will create a new norm for myself free of the pain and fear from the past.

It's a process, and it's hard. Every day I have to remind myself that I'm not that little girl anymore, that I don't have to live in that toxic environment, whether it's in my parents' house or in a relationship with a man who doesn't value me. I have to teach myself what healthy love looks like, and more importantly, that I'm worthy of it. It's a journey, and I'm not there yet, but I'm getting closer. And for now, that's enough.

Chapter: 24
Footprints in my life and on my heart

People come into our lives for certain reasons and times. Some people rush in and rush out, perhaps leaving a gouge in our hearts or only the faintest whisper of their time with us.

Some people stay with us, walk beside us for years, help us when we're down, cheer for us when we're on top, or just have a steady presence that continues to influence us if we are physically apart. Now, I'm going to share with you some of the people who have come into and impacted my life. 'Sarah'

Sarah came into my life at a time when I desperately needed someone like her—a true blessing in disguise. About 7-8 years ago, I grew close to her, the wife of one of my cousins, and from that point on, she became the older sister I had always dreamed of having. It's funny how life works sometimes, how people come into your life just when you need them most, and that's exactly what Sarah did for me. If it wasn't for my cousin marrying her, I honestly don't think I would have ever met her, and I can't imagine my life without her now.

Sarah is this fun, quirky, big-hearted woman who lights up any room she walks into. She's the type of person who goes above and beyond for the people she loves, and I can't even begin to describe how much she's done for me. During my darkest days—when I was super suicidal, drowning in family issues, and couldn't see a way out, she was the only one there for me. She was the one who wiped the tears from my face, who sat with me for hours, just listening as I vented about everything going wrong in my life, without a single judgment.

Sarah knows all my secrets, all my weaknesses. I've never kept anything from her because she's the one person I feel completely safe with. She's given me advice countless times, and even when I didn't take it, she never once said, "I told you so." She's held me in her arms more times than I can count, offering nothing but unconditional love. Sarah has welcomed me into her home, and she's even asked me to live with her multiple times. That offer alone meant the world to me, showing me just how much she cares.

What's truly remarkable about Sarah is her loyalty and discretion. Even though she's married to my cousin, I'm so much closer to her than I am to him. He doesn't know half the things that are going on in my life; in fact, I doubt he knows anything at all. But Sarah? She knows everything, and I do mean everything. In despite knowing everything, she's never once shared it with anyone—not even with her own husband. That's something I truly love and respect about her: her ability to keep my confidence, no matter what.

Sarah has done so much for me, and I don't think I could ever fully express how much she means to me or how deeply I love her. She's the type of friend everyone needs—someone who loves you unconditionally, without any judgments, and who's your ultimate ride or die. I can't imagine what my life would be like without her, and I honestly believe I would be lost if I ever lost her.

I know that the stories I've shared with Sarah have hurt her. I've seen her cry, not because she pities me, but because she can't fathom what it's like to walk in my shoes. She doesn't understand why life can be so unfair, why some people are tested in the worst ways. Sarah grew up in a loving home with parents who did everything for her, so my experiences are completely foreign to her. But even though she doesn't fully understand, she tries and I've seen the hurt in her eyes as she tries to wrap her mind around everything I've gone through.

Having Sarah in my life has made me realize the importance of having someone who truly cares, who's there for you through thick and thin, and who never judges you for the things you've been through. She's the sister I never had, and I'm beyond grateful to have her by my side. Sarah has always been the one to take care of me in every way imaginable. No matter the situation, she made sure I was okay, supported, and never felt alone.

Every birthday, she went out of her way to make sure it was a special day for me. Even if she didn't like the venues I picked or the food, she never complained. Instead, she would show up with a smile, ready to celebrate with me. One of my favorite memories is when she made me a tower cake out of donuts on my birthday. She gave me the biggest hug and treated me to an all-day spa experience, complete with a delicious lunch afterward. That was Sarah, always going above and beyond, making sure I felt loved and cherished.

Christmas was no different. Even though we technically didn't celebrate it, Sarah always made sure to get me thoughtful gifts. My favorite gift to this day is the fact that I get to borrow anything from her closet. Whether it's Chanel boots or a YSL purse, Sarah's wardrobe was open to me, and even if I didn't fit into her clothes perfectly, I made sure to make it work somehow.

It's those little gestures that showed me how much she cared, how much she wanted to be there for me in every way possible.

I remember a time when I was really struggling financially. I was basically the breadwinner for my family, and it was a huge responsibility that I didn't know how to handle. I was trying to figure out life, and I had no idea how to make ends meet, let alone how to make $10k a month. Asking my parents for help was out of the question because they needed help themselves. But Sarah? She always made sure I had money for gas and food. There were times when I was stuck at a gas station with no money and no gas, but Sarah would always come through. She never made me feel bad for asking for help, even when I was embarrassed and felt like I was taking blows to my pride. She never threw it in my face or made me feel ashamed for needing support. It took me a while to learn how to put my pride aside and ask for help when I needed it. But Sarah taught me that it's okay to ask for help, that it's okay to lean on someone when life gets tough. She was always there, never judging, never making me feel less than, even when I couldn't pay her back. I felt guilty at times for always needing her help, but she never let me feel that way for a long. She would brush it off, reminding me that she was there for me, no matter what.

I hope everyone has or finds a person like Sarah. She is a rare soul, a true gem in this world, and I am so incredibly grateful for her. She's the sister I never had but always needed, and I can't imagine my life without her. Sarah's presence in my life has been nothing short of a blessing, and I know that no matter what, she'll always be there for me, just as I'll always be there for her.

To my Sarah, I love you so much! Thank you for everything you have done for me. I would be lost without you, and my cousin is beyond lucky to have a wife like you. Your children don't realize how blessed they are to have a mother like you. When the time comes when I get married and have children of my own, just know I hope to be at least half the person you are, and I will definitely be dropping them off at your house for babysitting, especially for those overnight stays, lol.

You are my rock, my guiding light, and the sister I never knew I needed. Thank you for being my everything and for reassuring me that, in life, I need to keep fighting and never fear anything or anyone. I love you more than words can express, and I'm forever grateful to have you in my life.

Drita

Growing up, I had a friend named Drita. We met in the 7th grade and stayed close all the way into adulthood. Our bond was strong, and I always thought we would be in each other's lives forever, raising our kids together and sharing those precious milestones. But life had different plans for us.

Drita got married when she was just 18 years old, and soon after, she had a son. I was thrilled for her, but it also marked the beginning of our paths diverging. Despite the changes, I held onto the belief that we would remain inseparable. After all, Drita was more than just a friend; she was like a sister to me. I was even honored to be the maid of honor at her wedding, a role I cherished because it felt like a celebration of our deep connection.

However, there was always tension between our families. My mom, in particular, couldn't stand Drita. She would constantly tell me that she got bad vibes from her and that I should stay away.

But one thing about me is that I don't let anyone, not even my parents, dictate who I can and can't be friends with. I'm fiercely loyal to the people I care about, and I will stand up for them no matter what. So, I brushed off my mom's concerns and continued to be there for Drita, no matter what.

When Drita got married, she moved away to San Francisco to be with her husband and his family. That was really hard for me because the physical distance put a strain on our friendship. But what made it even worse was that her husband wasn't a good person. He cheated on Drita repeatedly, and when she became pregnant, she wasn't ready to be a mother. Yet, her husband forced her to have the baby, leaving her feeling trapped.

I felt bad for Drita for a long time because I could see how unhappy she was. No matter how much she tried to leave her husband, he would always find ways to pull her back. I couldn't understand why she would keep going back to him. It frustrated me to no end. But as I got older, I began to understand. Drita was doing what she thought was best for her son. She would do anything for his happiness, even if it meant sacrificing her own.

Her son adored his father despite all the turmoil. And when her son was diagnosed with autism, Drita stepped up in ways that amazed me. She poured everything she had into helping her son, making sure he had all the support and resources he needed. Her dedication to him was unwavering, even when it meant putting her own needs last.

Our friendship began to change as Drita's life became more centered around her family. We weren't as close as we used to be, and the distance between us grew, not just physically but emotionally. I struggled to accept that our lives were taking such different paths, but I always hoped that somehow we would find our way back to each other.

In the end, life didn't play out the way I had imagined. The distance, the challenges, and the pressures of our separate lives created a gap that couldn't be bridged. It's a hard reality to face, losing someone who was once so integral to your life. But I'll always hold onto the memories of the times we shared, the laughter, the secrets, and the dreams we had for our future. Drita will always have a special place in my heart, no matter where life takes us.

When Drita finally left her husband for good and moved back to Los Angeles, I was filled with mixed emotions. On one hand, I was overjoyed to have my best friend back, the person who had been like a sister to me for so many years. On the other hand, I was deeply saddened by the circumstances she was facing. Starting over with no money, as a single mother to an autistic child was a daunting challenge. Her son's condition was severe, he would have intense, violent tantrums, breaking things and hitting anyone near him. He couldn't speak or communicate effectively, which only added to his frustration and made the outbursts even more frequent.

I tried my best to support Drita through this difficult time. Despite my own financial struggles, I did what I could to help her out, offering her rides whenever she needed to go somewhere, and even trying to assist her financially. Her ex-husband, unfortunately, was a complete deadbeat. He had no interest in contributing to his son's care or being a present father. His visits were rare and fleeting, showing up once every few months for a day or two and then disappearing again. It was heartbreaking to see Drita trying to manage everything on her own, especially in such a challenging situation.

Our friendship, however, didn't end because of distance or growing apart, it ended because of the constant backstabbing and the toxic patterns Drita couldn't break free from. Whenever she started dating someone new, she would put on this facade, pretending to be someone she wasn't. She would lie about who she was, presenting herself as this perfect, flawless person. I couldn't stand the fakeness. I always believed that if someone couldn't accept you for who you truly are, then they weren't worth your time. But Drita didn't see it that way. She played these men, leading them on, and it bothered me. I would always tell her to be honest, to stop playing games because many of the men she was dealing with didn't deserve the crap she was giving them.

Two years after her separation, Drita finally met someone new, a decent Middle Eastern man who accepted her for who she was, including her son. I was thrilled for her. I thought maybe, just maybe, this was her chance to have the happiness she had been searching for. I loved that he seemed to care for her son, even treating him as his own. But as time went on, I began to see the cracks in the facade. This new man, Kyle, turned out to be ten times worse than her first husband.

Kyle wasn't just a cheater or a womanizer; he was a manipulative, controlling narcissist. He wanted to control every aspect of Drita's life, where she went, who she was with, everything. If she didn't answer her phone, he would call her nonstop until she did. He isolated her from her friends and family, including me. He manipulated her into believing whatever he wanted, turning her against the people who truly cared about her. He made her cut ties with anyone he deemed a threat to his control, and Drita, unfortunately, fell for it.

When Drita began to distance herself from me, it was clear that Kyle had succeeded in driving a wedge between us. Our friendship, which had spanned over a decade, was being destroyed by this man's toxicity. It was exhausting, draining, and it broke my heart. But at the same time, I was relieved when our friendship ended. I didn't want to be in a relationship, even a friendship, where I had to constantly prove my worth and loyalty. I believe in mutual respect and trust, and that was no longer present in our relationship.

A few months later, I found out that Drita had married Kyle. Despite everything, I genuinely hoped that she would finally find the happiness she deserved. But it wasn't long before I heard that her second marriage had ended in divorce after less than five months. It was sad, but I knew that I couldn't allow her back into my life. No matter how much pain someone is in, if they are willing to throw away a 15-year friendship for a man, then they aren't someone I want in my life.

Drita made her choices, and I made mine. After trying to prove myself trustworthy to Drita over and over, I started to doubt if I was even good enough for any friendship. Her choices left shadows on my heart, causing me to be cautious of allowing anyone else as close to me as she once was. I chose to protect my peace and my well-being, and I've learned that it's okay to walk away from people who no longer bring positivity into your life, no matter how much history you share.

Moe I took a deep breath and sat back down, trying to process everything Moe had just told me. We hadn't been dating long, just a few months. I was learning to be more discerning about the men I chose to be in my life, but I never saw this coming. The air felt thick with tension, and I could feel my heart racing. Part of me wanted to run, to put as much distance as possible between myself and the situation, but another part of me knew that I couldn't just abandon him in his moment of need. We had grown close over the past few months, and I genuinely cared for him. Despite the gravity of his revelation, I had to remind myself that accusations aren't the same as convictions.

Moe continued to speak, his voice shaky and uneven, as he explained the situation in more detail. He told me that he had met the woman through mutual friends and that they had gone out a few times, but according to him, nothing ever happened between them. He insisted that the accusation was a misunderstanding, perhaps even an attempt to extort money from him and that he was terrified of how it might ruin his life.

As I listened to him, I couldn't help but think back to my own experiences, the trauma I had endured, and how it shaped the way I viewed the world. I knew all too well the devastating impact of sexual assault, and it made me question everything. How could I, a victim myself, reconcile my feelings for Moe with the possibility that he could be guilty of such a crime?

I asked Moe to tell me more about the events leading up to the accusation, trying to gauge whether there was anything in his story that didn't add up. He explained that the woman had started acting strangely after their last date, sending him erratic messages and making unusual demands. Moe said he had tried to cut off contact with her, but she became increasingly hostile, eventually leading to the accusation.

As he spoke, I could see the pain and fear in his eyes. Moe wasn't just worried about the legal consequences, he was also deeply concerned about how this would affect his reputation, his relationships, and his future. He kept repeating that he couldn't understand why she would do

this to him, that he had never been anything but kind to her. I wanted to believe him. I wanted to believe that the man I had grown so fond of was telling me the truth, that he was innocent. But at the same time, I knew I couldn't ignore the possibility that there might be more to the story than he was letting on.

At that moment, I felt a deep conflict within myself. On one hand, I was the compassionate friend, the person who wanted to be there for him and support him through this ordeal. On the other hand, I was a survivor who knew the importance of believing victims. It was a difficult balance to strike, and I found myself grappling with a flood of emotions.

After he finished explaining, Moe looked at me with pleading eyes, waiting for my response. I could see the desperation in his expression, the silent hope that I would stand by him, that I would be the one person who didn't judge him based on the accusation alone.

"Moe," I said softly, "I don't know what to say. This is a lot to take in, and I need some time to process everything." He nodded, his shoulders slumping slightly as if he had been expecting that answer. "I understand," he replied, his voice barely above a whisper. "I just didn't know who else to turn to. You're the only person I trust."

We sat in silence for a few moments, the weight of the situation pressing down on both of us. I reached out and took his hand, trying to convey some semblance of comfort even though my own mind was in turmoil. "I'm here for you," I told him, "but I need to figure out how I feel about all of this."

That night, I left Moe's apartment with a heavy heart. I had no idea what the future held for us or how this revelation would change the dynamic of our relationship. All I knew was that I needed time, time to think, time to sort through my emotions, and time to decide what the next steps should be. As I drove home, the city lights blurring past me, I couldn't shake the feeling that my world had just been turned upside down.

The news of Moe's arrest hit me like a ton of bricks. I was at home, going about my day when I received a call from our mutual friends. When they told me what had happened, my mind went blank for a moment. It was as if the world around me stopped. I could barely process what they were saying. Moe, the man I had spent so much time with, who I had trusted, was now in jail for raping two women. My stomach churned, and I felt a wave of nausea wash over me. How could this be true? The man I knew couldn't possibly be capable of something so vile, so horrific.

But the reality was staring me in the face. The women had come forward, and their stories were consistent. They had been drugged at the club, and both had woken up in Moe's bed with no memory of what had happened. The hospital had confirmed their worst fears, they had been raped. The evidence was damning, and it left no room for doubt. Moe was guilty.

I felt a surge of anger, not just at Moe but at myself as well. How could I have been so blind?

What clues had I missed? How could I have let myself believe him when he told me that he wasn't capable of such a thing? I had trusted him, I had defended him, and now I felt betrayed in the worst possible way. The man I had once cared for had turned out to be a monster, and I was disgusted with myself for ever thinking otherwise.

When his family reached out to me, asking me to testify on his behalf, I was livid. They wanted me to stand up in court and vouch for his character, to tell the judge and jury what a good man he was, how he could never have committed such a crime. But I knew the truth, and there was no way I was going to lie to him. I wasn't going to be complicit in allowing a predator to walk free. I thought about the victims, the women whose lives had been shattered by Moe's actions. I thought about the trauma they must be going through, the pain and fear they would carry with them for the rest of their lives. And I thought about how I had been so close to being one of them. It made me sick to my core.

I told his family that I would not testify for him, that I would not write a letter of support. I refused to be part of any effort to free him. Moe had made his choices, and now he had to face the consequences. There was no excuse for what he had done, and he deserved to be behind bars. I wanted him to stay in jail for as long as possible. I wanted him to pay for the pain he had caused.

As I hung up the phone, I felt a sense of closure. It wasn't easy, but I knew I had made the right decision. I had to stand up for what was right, even if it meant going against someone I once cared about. Moe had betrayed my trust and violated the trust of those women in the most horrific way. There was no forgiveness for that, no redemption.

I didn't feel sorry for him. I didn't pity him. All I felt was relief that he was finally where he belonged, away from society, where he couldn't hurt anyone else. I vowed to never allow myself to be so easily deceived again. I would be stronger, more cautious, and I would never let anyone take advantage of my trust the way Moe had.

In the end, I realized that my strength lay in my ability to stand up for what was right, even when it was difficult, even when it hurt. I had to protect not just myself but others from people like Moe. And I would carry that lesson with me for the rest of my life.

Chapter: 25
Hindsight is 20/20

Looking back, I see how much I craved validation from others to define my worth. When people didn't like me, I automatically assumed there was something inherently wrong with me. I believed I was flawed, inadequate, and unworthy of love. It wasn't just about being accepted; it was about fitting in, about being seen, and about being enough for those around me. I became a people-pleaser, constantly bending over backward to make others happy, even if it meant sacrificing my own well-being.

The twisted part is that even when people hurt me, I was the one apologizing. I felt like I needed to beg for their forgiveness just to keep them in my life. It didn't matter if they broke me, used me, or walked all over me, I was okay with it because I was so desperate not to be alone. I know now how unhealthy that was, but back then, I didn't know any better. I had no self-confidence, no self-respect, and no clue how to even start building those things. The word "No" wasn't in my vocabulary. I was always saying "Yes," even when I knew deep down it would cost me. I just wanted to be cool, to be liked, to feel like I belonged somewhere.

Growing up, school was a nightmare. I wasn't a pretty girl, and I definitely wasn't popular. I was tall, dark-skinned, and chunky, with a Dora the Explorer haircut that did me no favors. Every day during lunch, the kids would chant "Unibrow" at me. Yes, I had one eyebrow, and apparently, that made me the ultimate target for ridicule. This went on for years, all the way until high school. Even then, I wasn't the hot chick. I wasn't in any cliques, and people just didn't like me. I felt invisible, like I was just there, existing in the background.

But then something changed after high school. When I went to college, it was like I transformed. The glow-up was real, and suddenly, I was one of the popular girls. It was surreal. I went from being the outcast to the girl everyone wanted to hang out with. It felt amazing—finally, the attention I had always craved was mine. I know it sounds crazy, but for someone who had never been loved or had friends, suddenly being adored and sought after was intoxicating.

As I got older, though, I started to realize that having a huge group of friends wasn't as great as it seemed. In fact, it was one of the worst things because most of those people were only around for the good times. When things got dark, when life got tough, they vanished. They didn't want to deal with my problems or hear about my struggles.

One of the hardest lessons I've learned is that not everyone who pretends to care actually does. Some people just want to know everything about you so they can use that information against you later. They'll listen to your deepest secrets only to spread rumors and hurt you when you least expect it. I've been hurt a lot in my life, and those experiences taught me the importance of keeping my circle small and tight.

Not everyone needs to know what's going on in your life, especially your love life. There are evil people out there, people who will take advantage of your vulnerability. Even those you consider friends can betray you. That's why it's crucial to surround yourself with people you can 100% rely on, those who have seen you at your worst and still stick around. The ones who check on you daily, who are there for you through thick and thin. If you're lucky enough to have friendships like that, cherish them. Work through your fights and arguments because good souls with pure intentions are incredibly rare to find.

Star

Two years ago, Drita was hosting a baby shower for her sister-in-law, and she invited me to the event. My parents never liked Drita or her family and really didn't want me to go, but, as always, I fought my way with them and ended up attending. Drita had a knack for throwing and hosting events. If there was one thing she excelled at, it was creating lavish parties that left everyone in awe. She would craft everything by hand, from decorations to party favors, making everything look as though it had come straight from a professional vendor.

That night at the party, I unexpectedly ran into an old friend, Star. We went way back, but as we grew older, life had taken us in different directions, causing us to drift apart. It wasn't because of any fight or disagreement; we were simply in different chapters of our lives. I remembered that Star's parents had gotten engaged at my aunt's house years ago, and back then, Star was really close with my older cousin.

Seeing Star that night was like a breath of fresh air. We couldn't stop laughing and reminiscing about the old days. It was so nice reconnecting with her that it made me realize how much I had missed her. A couple of days after the party, I decided to reach out to her, and we made plans to grab lunch together. That lunch marked the beginning of rekindling our friendship, and it felt like picking up right where we had left off.

When things went south with Drita, I made the difficult decision to end our friendship once and for all. Around the same time, Star and I became really close again, and we both ended up cutting ties with Drita and her sister. Since then, Star and I have been inseparable. We talked every day, multiple times a day, from morning until evening, and we made time to see each other regularly. Our friendship blossomed into something special, and I loved her like a little sister. She came to my home many times, and my family adored her.

Star has such a great soul and a loving heart, but there's one thing to know about her: she is very ruthless. She doesn't have a filter and will tell you exactly how it is, even if it's harsh. She speaks her mind and doesn't care how you take it or how it makes you feel. There were times when Star's sharp words wounded me, and she made me cry because of how brutally honest she was. She knew my weaknesses and could easily push my buttons, but I would still forgive her. I never overstepped with Star; I just learned how to tolerate her personality and understood where she was coming from. I valued our friendship despite the occasional hurtful moments because I knew that beneath her tough exterior, she cared deeply about me. Star's bluntness was part of who she was, and while it wasn't always easy to hear, I knew she meant well. Our bond grew stronger because we were honest with each other, even when it hurt.

Star and I never argued or got into fights because we genuinely understood each other. We had a bond that was built on mutual respect and a deep understanding of each other's personalities and struggles. I have to say, Star was there for me during some of the darkest days of my life. When James screwed me over, Star stood by me, unwavering in her support. I'll never forget the day I found out he was having a child with someone else. I felt like my world was falling apart, and I cried my eyes out in the car, screaming and yelling, trying to comprehend why he would do something so hurtful. Star didn't just sit there; she held me in her arms and reassured me that everything would be okay. She told me that James loved me and that we would work things out. At that moment, I felt the depth of her care and the sincerity of her words. I knew that Star only had good intentions for me. She was like a sister, always ready to pick me up when I was down, and I trusted her completely.

As time went on, my relationships with both Henry and James deteriorated. They both caused me immense pain and each time I felt broken, Star was there to pick up the pieces. She had my back, no questions asked. However, something always nagged at the back of my mind: everyone kept telling me to be cautious about letting Star too deeply into my life, always to have some kind of guard up. But I couldn't believe that. If someone was going to be a part of my life, especially someone I saw and talked to every day, there shouldn't be any secrets or jealousy between us. I believed that true friendship meant being open, honest, and trusting.

Yet, there was something about Star's actions that I couldn't quite understand. When Henry and I stopped talking, she knew how deeply it affected me. It felt like a part of me was missing, and she saw how much it hurt. Despite this, she would still greet Henry and talk to him whenever she saw him. I never understood why. Why did she feel the need to be cordial with Henry when Henry and I weren't together? And why did she have such disdain for James? She hated James so much that she even tried to put him in jail, but with Henry, it was a different story.

Star is the type of person whose words can cut deep; she's never holding back, even if it means hurting someone's feelings. She's brutally honest, sometimes to the point of being insensitive, and she's unapologetic about it. I've seen her bring people to tears, myself included, with her harsh critiques and blunt opinions. She's not the type to sugarcoat anything, and while that can be refreshing in a world full of people who avoid the truth, it can also be incredibly painful.

Despite her cold exterior and her often harsh words, I've come to understand that this is just who Star is. She doesn't mean to hurt people; she just doesn't have the filter most people do. She'll say what's on her mind, regardless of how it might come across. There have been times when her words have cut me to the core, leaving me questioning my self-worth or doubting my decisions.

Yet, I always knew that she wasn't trying to be cruel; she just didn't see the need to soften the blow.

There's a part of me that admires her for that. Star is unapologetically herself, and in a way, that's something I've always strived to be. She's strong, independent, and doesn't care about pleasing others, which is something I've struggled with my whole life. She was my rock, even though her way of supporting me was tough love. But with that strength comes a lack of empathy that can be hard to deal with, especially when you're going through something difficult and need a friend to lean on. I noticed that Star's coldness wasn't just reserved for moments of brutal honesty. She would be dismissive of my feelings at times, acting as if I was being overly dramatic or weak for feeling the way I did. If I ever brought up how her words or actions hurt me, she would brush it off, never apologizing or acknowledging that she had crossed a line. It was as if she couldn't see or didn't care, how her behavior affected me.

This coldness extended beyond just our interactions. Both Henry and James had done the same awful things to me. They lied, betrayed, and broke me down. So why couldn't Star have them the same way? It was confusing and, in a way, hurtful to see how she treated them unequally. I wanted her to be on my side, to see things the way I did, but for some reason, she couldn't bring herself to treat Henry the same way she treated James. It was one of those things that I couldn't wrap my head around, and it left a lingering sense of unease in our friendship. It felt like a betrayal, but I never confronted her about it. Maybe I was afraid of what she might say, or maybe I just didn't want to lose another person in my life.

Loving someone like Star from a distance has become a necessary act of self-preservation how she treated me of how my father treated me as a child, always putting me down and making me feel worthless. Her actions and words were gouging my heart and started to trigger my PTSD. I felt like I was going backwards in my journey to healing from the trauma of my past. I care about her deeply, but I also know that I need to protect myself from the aspects of her personality that can be damaging. I've learned that it's okay to set boundaries, even with people you love. It's okay to step back when someone's behavior starts to negatively impact your well-being. I still cherish the moments when Star and I can laugh and enjoy each other's company, but I no longer allow her to have the same influence over me as she once did. I've come to realize that it's possible to love someone and keep them at arm's length, especially when the relationship has elements that are toxic. I refuse to let anyone, even someone as important to me as Star, disrespect or belittle me. My self-worth is too valuable to allow anyone to tear it down, no matter how much I care for them.

Zee

Growing up with my cousin Zee was like having a built-in best friend. We were inseparable, and it felt like we were sisters more than cousins. Since she was my only cousin on my dad's side, and she lived just five minutes away, we spent nearly every day together. From Pre-K all the way to junior high, we attended the same school, which meant we walked home together every day, sharing stories and laughs along the way.

Zee was everything I wanted to be. She was the epitome of the perfect student—straight A's, never in trouble, always impressing the teachers and her parents. I, on the other hand, struggled to keep up. I wasn't a bad student, but compared to Zee, I always felt like I was falling short. Her parents doted on her, giving her everything she wanted, and sometimes, I couldn't help but wish that they would adopt me too. It wasn't that my parents didn't care, but there was something about the way Zee was treated that made me long for that same kind of unconditional support and admiration.

We had this unspoken routine after school that became a comforting ritual. As soon as we got home, we'd head straight to the kitchen. If her mom hadn't already prepared something for us, we'd fix ourselves a snack—usually something simple like a Hot Pocket or a frozen pizza. Then, we'd plop down in front of the TV and dive into our favorite shows. Despite our age, we were obsessed with "Ugly Betty" and "Desperate Housewives." Looking back, it's funny to think about two young girls being so engrossed in those shows, but Zee's parents were pretty laid-back about what we watched.

After a couple of hours of indulging in our TV time, it was down to business. We'd head to her room, where we'd start on our homework. Zee was always so disciplined; she liked to have music playing while she studied, something that drove me crazy. I needed complete silence to focus, especially when it came to schoolwork. Math was my nemesis, and no matter how much I tried, the numbers never seemed to add up right in my head. Zee, on the other hand, excelled in every subject. She was patient with me, always offering to help with my math homework, explaining things in a way that sometimes made it click, but other times, just made me feel more frustrated. But I appreciated her efforts, and in those moments, I admired her even more.

Being around Zee pushed me to be better, even if I couldn't always meet the high standards she seemed to set so effortlessly. I wanted to be just like her, to have that same confidence and success in school. But more than anything, I cherished the bond we shared. It was more than just studying together or watching TV. It was the sense of belonging, of having someone who understood me in a way that no one else did. With Zee, I never felt alone, and that was the most important thing of all.

Zee and I shared a bond that was as complex as it was close. While we were practically inseparable, our relationship had its peculiar dynamics, dynamics that were largely dictated by Zee's knack for manipulating situations to her advantage. Being three months older than me, she always seemed to have the upper hand, and she knew exactly how to wield that power. Looking back, it's almost comical how much control she had over me. I was scared of her in that way, kids are scared of someone who just seems to know how to get them into trouble.

One time, when we were much younger, I accidentally let the F-word slip. For a kid, that's a big deal—one of those words you know would get you into serious trouble if the adults found out. Zee, of course, seized the opportunity. Anytime I tried to stand up to her or refuse one of her demands, she would casually threaten, "Uncle, did you know, one day, Sam said the F-word?"

The mere mention of that would send me running to her side, ready to agree to whatever she wanted, just so she wouldn't rat me out. It wasn't that her demands were outrageous; she mostly just wanted me to do her bidding, to be her little servant. And somehow, it always worked. She had me wrapped around her finger, and I couldn't do anything about it.

Zee also had two older brothers, who played their own roles in our childhood antics. The eldest brother, being much older, was more like a second dad to us. We didn't dare mess with him, he was strict and always in charge. But the middle brother, Joe, was a different story. Joe was eight years older than us and loved to mess with us, which, in hindsight, was just his way of showing affection, even if it was a bit twisted.

One particular day stands out. Our parents had to go to some event, and Joe was left in charge of watching us. Now, Joe had a reputation for being a bit of a prankster, and we were wary of what he might come up with. As soon as our parents left, Joe saw his chance. He asked Zee and me to go down to the basement, where the laundry room was, to grab a shirt for him. We obeyed, not wanting to get on Joe's bad side. But as soon as we stepped into the basement, Joe locked the door behind us and wouldn't let us back upstairs. We were trapped in the cold, dark basement, and panic set in.

Luckily, Zee had the house phone in her hand. We opened the garage door and started screaming, telling Joe that if he didn't let us out, we'd call our parents and tell them what he did. At first, Joe didn't believe we'd actually go through with it. But then Zee started dialing, and he saw that we weren't bluffing. Joe raced down the stairs to unlock the door, but he wasn't going to let us off the hook that easily. He tried shoving us into the dryer, thinking it would be hilarious, but we were two little, stubby girls with Dora the Explorer haircuts, and there was no way we were fitting in there. That was Joe's way of showing love—he didn't really want to hurt us; he just thought we were annoying like any older brother would.

Another time, Joe had a crush on a girl from his high school and wanted to impress her. Naturally, our parents left us in his care again. Joe invited the girl over, and I remember being surprised because I had never seen him go to such lengths for anyone before. He actually prepared a cheese plate and opened a bottle of wine— things I had never seen him do. They sat on the patio, chatting and enjoying their makeshift date. But then Joe's mom called, saying she was on her way back home. Joe panicked. He had no idea how to get the girl to leave without raising suspicions. So, he turned to us for help. He asked Zee and me to fake cry and pretend we got hurt or something, just to create a distraction. As always, we did what he asked. We cried and whined, and Joe quickly cleaned up, washing the wine glasses and tidying everything up as if nothing had happened. He was clever, always finding a way to get away with things.

My childhood with Zee and Joe was filled with these kinds of moments, ridiculous, funny, and sometimes a little scary. Despite the odd power dynamics and the pranks, these memories are precious to me. They shaped our relationship and created a bond that, despite its quirks, was built on love, trust, and the shared experiences of growing up together.

Zee and I have always loved playing in the hair salon when we were bored. It was one of those activities that felt so innocent and fun, especially since Zee had this incredible mane of long, black hair that went past her waist. One day, feeling a little more adventurous than usual, I decided to use real scissors instead of our usual play tools. I wasn't paying attention, lost in our pretend world, when I accidentally cut off half of Zee's hair on one side.

The moment I realized what I had done, panic set in. I looked down at the chunk of hair in my hand, and it felt like time stopped.

I was so scared of what would happen next, knowing how much Zee loved her long hair. Without missing a beat, Zee ran downstairs to tell her mom, and as luck would have it, my dad was there too. Both of our parents came rushing upstairs, their faces a mix of shock and anger. They started yelling at us immediately. Zee got a slap on the butt for allowing me to use real scissors and was locked in her parents' room as a punishment.

My dad, on the other hand, was furious. He slapped me hard across the face and locked me in Joe's room, where he shared space with his eldest brother. I was told I wasn't allowed to leave the room, no matter what. After some time, I really needed to use the bathroom, but I was too scared to ask for permission. I tried my best to hold it in, but I was just seven years old, there was only so much I could do. Eventually, I couldn't hold it any longer and ended up peeing in my pants, all over the floor of Joe's bedroom.

When Joe came home from school later that day, he had no idea what had happened. He opened his bedroom door to find me standing there, covered in pee, the evidence of my punishment all over his floor. Joe was livid. He started yelling and screaming, asking the parents how they could let me pee in his room. I couldn't stop crying; I was humiliated and scared, and the whole situation felt so unfair.

At the moment, it was anything but funny, but now, looking back, we can't help but laugh about it. It's one of those stories that gets retold at family gatherings, with everyone shaking their heads in disbelief that I actually chopped Zee's hair off. It's a memory that reminds me of the innocence of childhood and how even the most stressful situations can eventually turn into something we laugh about years later.

Zee was always into yoga and embraced that whole hippie lifestyle. It was never really my thing, but I was always down to try anything with her if it meant spending time together. As we got older, life started to pull us in different directions. We both got busy with our own lives, so we tried to at least hang out every couple of months, but we still made it a point to call or text each other every other day. Zee had started working at a country club, and she loved it. She was making more money than most college students at the time, meeting a lot of cool people, and making new friends. I was genuinely happy for her, but as time went by, she started getting more and more distant. I wasn't sure what was going on. I thought maybe she was just getting really busy.

One day, we went for a hike. Zee loved hiking and knew some of the coolest spots. But that day, she was unusually quiet. I kept asking her what was going on, but she just brushed it off. Finally, as we reached a secluded part of the trail, she stopped walking and started to cry. She told me she had been keeping a secret from me, something that was tearing her apart. I was shocked and confused, not understanding what could be so bad that she felt the need to hide it from me. I stopped walking too, and just held her. I told her that whatever it was, we would get through it together.

It took her a while to start talking. She said that what she was about to tell me might trigger me, and I tried to stay calm, reassuring her that I would be okay. Then she told me what had happened. Her job had been making her work the night shift a lot lately, and one day, after her shift was over, she was walking to her car alone in the pitch dark. As she tried to get into her car, a male coworker, who was drunk, forced himself onto her and raped her.

My heart dropped when I heard that. I couldn't believe what I was hearing. I didn't know how to respond or what to do. All I could do was hold her in my arms and cry with her. I asked if she had told anyone about the situation. Zee told me she had been silent for almost seven months, and that she had to see the man almost every day. She was afraid to tell anyone, and I understood her pain.

Zee explained that she had started seeing a therapist, and it was helping her a little. She even changed her work schedule so she wouldn't have to see that guy anymore. She forced her parents to go to therapy with her because she wanted to tell them what had happened. I respected her so much for that because it took incredible strength to share something so horrific with her parents. As time went on, I made more of an effort to be there for her. I wanted Zee to know that I understood her pain and that I would do everything I could to support her through this. I told her that she wasn't alone in her journey of healing, and that she would always have me by her side. The whole experience brought us closer together, and it reminded me of how important it is to be there for the people you care about, especially in their darkest moments.

It's beautiful to see how Zee's journey brought her back to herself and led her to find true happiness. Watching her thrive, move out on her own, and live her life to the fullest was inspiring. When she started working at that famous restaurant in LA, I could tell it was a turning point for her. The way she met her now-husband, who was not just the owner but the main chef of the restaurant, felt like something out of a movie. Their connection was immediate, and it was clear that they were meant for each other.

They didn't just work together; they built something together. Zee's natural talent in the kitchen shone through as her husband often invited her to work alongside him. She had a way of making everything she touched taste like it was made by a professional chef. Whether it was a simple dish or something more elaborate, Zee could whip it up from scratch, and it would taste like it was straight out of a five-star restaurant.

After dating for about a year, Zee finally introduced him to me. I was so excited to meet the man who made her so happy, and I wasn't disappointed. He was everything I could have hoped for her: kind, supportive, and clearly in love with my cousin. I could see it in the way he looked at her and in the way she smiled around him— she was genuinely happy.

Chapter: 26
Understanding My Dad or Trying to…

Our relationship felt stronger than ever during this time, but naturally, things changed when Zee got married. Her life became busier with the responsibilities of marriage and managing her husband's three restaurants. While my family wasn't invited to her wedding, the photos I saw and accounts the rest of the family shared showed me it was a beautiful day for her. After the wedding, she had a lot on her plate, and while we did drift apart, and even if it felt like she was abandoning me for her new life, there was no love lost between us. I understood that her priorities had shifted, and I was just happy to see her living a life that brought her joy and fulfillment.

Even though our childhood was overshadowed by manipulation and our struggles for acknowledgment and love from our parents, Zee was there for me during my darkest days, and I'll always cherish that. Our bond goes beyond blood, it's built on shared experiences and the love we've shown each other over the years. Even though we may not be as close as we once were, the memories we created growing up together will always be a part of me. I'm grateful for the time we had and for the knowledge that, no matter what, Zee will always be someone I can count on.

Understanding

The hardships I went through with my parents were difficult, but one thing I can say is that I am grateful for them because they made me who I am today. If it wasn't for falling to rock bottom numerous times, I wouldn't be this strong, independent woman. Don't get me wrong, I still struggle. My life is nowhere near perfect. I still have my hard days, and I've learned to ask for help when needed. I've learned who I can and cannot trust. I also realized that my parents, in their own way, only wanted the best for me, even when I couldn't see it and resisted them.

Somehow, I've learned to forgive my parents for all the shit they put me through, even though we've never spoken about it.

I've accepted that my parents will never change, but I can—and I can write my own story. I've learned that I don't need anyone's validation, and I definitely don't need to be a people pleaser. Saying "NO" is completely fine. I don't need to go above and beyond for people who don't value me. I'm okay with being alone, and I'm okay with truly just loving myself, even when others don't. I've found strength in my vulnerability, and I've embraced the fact that my journey is uniquely mine.

About two years ago, my relationship with my father started to improve. He became more loving toward me and actually wanted to help me out in life. Don't misunderstand me or the situation, I was still very scared of him, so it was really hard to open up to him and trust him with anything because I was afraid he might lash out and hit me. My dad hasn't laid hands on me in many years, but the fear was always there.

I tried to be a daddy's girl, to accept the love my dad was now offering, but I felt like it was just too late. I didn't know how to repair that relationship with him, and I definitely didn't know how to bring up a conversation and ask why he never loved me and was so brutal with me. I had to learn to let the past go, to accept that he was trying, and to try to meet him in the middle. But it was extremely hard. I didn't know how to hug or kiss him, or even how to say, "Hey, Dad, I miss you."

Every time I tried to hug my dad, it just didn't feel right. I didn't feel a warm and loving feeling from him unless he was drunk; then he would hug and kiss me, and I could feel the love, even though I couldn't reciprocate the same feelings. I still didn't trust him, but as

I grew up, I knew that in order for me to be truly happy, I had to stop living in my father's shadow and stop trying to please him.

I felt like my father should have always been proud of me, no matter what the situation was, because, after all, I was his only child who sacrificed her whole life for my parents. I gave up my childhood and my social life to do everything I could to make them both happy. When my father needed money, I always found a way to give it to him, even when I was super broke. I made sure to always make him feel like he could count on me to be there for him and help him out when he needed it. Despite all that I did, I still struggled with the feeling that no matter what, it was never enough, and that deep down, the love between us would always be tainted by the past.

The memory of that day when my father punished me for not being able to say the number four in Farsi has always stayed with me. I was just five years old, innocent and eager to learn, but that one mistake cost me dearly. My father, in his anger, decided that the appropriate punishment was to lock me out on the patio in the freezing rain. I was only wearing a tee shirt and shorts, shivering and soaked to the bone. He left me out there for four hours, and worse still, he left me home alone. I remember standing out there, my tiny body shaking with cold and fear, crying out to God for help. The sky was dark, the rain was relentless, and I felt utterly abandoned. I can still feel the cold seeping into my bones, the helplessness of that little girl who didn't understand why her father was doing this to her.

When my mother finally came home and found me outside, she was furious. She and my father had a massive fight, her voice filled with anger and disbelief that he could do something so cruel.

I'll never forget how, later that night, I woke up screaming the number four in Farsi, over and over again. It became a symbol of the trauma that day caused me, a number that still brings back the fear and pain of that experience, even though we laugh about it now that I'm older. But no amount of laughter can erase the memory of how I felt, the lasting impact it had on me, or the trauma it inflicted.

Things only got worse when my father returned from Afghanistan. My life, which had been somewhat peaceful in his absence, was thrown into turmoil. He came back with severe PTSD, his anger was more intense than ever, and his behavior was more erratic. The man who had once punished me so harshly for a simple mistake now brought a whole new level of chaos into our lives. He would wake up screaming in the middle of the night, haunted by nightmares that none of us could understand. I begged him to seek help, to talk to someone, but he refused. Being old school, he didn't believe in therapy or counseling. Instead, he turned to liquor, drowning his pain in alcohol, thinking it would help him forget.

His anger became a constant presence in our home, especially toward my mother. He blamed her for everything, particularly for the financial mess we were in. He didn't seem to grasp that while he was gone, we were the ones left to pick up the pieces, to pay off his debts, to keep things afloat. When he came back, he decided that we needed to buy a house, and for six long months, my mother and I went house hunting, hoping that this would finally bring some peace. But even when we found a house and bought it, there was no peace. My father's anger only grew. He blamed my mother for every little thing, from the problems with the house to the fact that she didn't ask for help. It was as if nothing she did was ever good enough, and it broke my heart to see her treated this way.

I hated that house. I hated going home, knowing what awaited me there. Every night was a battle to avoid the inevitable chaos. I would drive around for hours, waiting for the lights to go out, hoping that by the time I got home, my parents would be asleep and the house would be quiet.

But more often than not, I would walk in to find plates being thrown, the sounds of screaming, and the sight of my father hitting my mother. It gave me the worst anxiety, to the point where I would lock myself in the bathroom, the only place in the house where I felt remotely safe. I would sit in the corner, hugging my knees, tears streaming down my face as I tried to block out the sounds of violence that filled the air. The bathroom became my sanctuary, a place where I could momentarily escape the nightmare that my life had become.

Seeing my father beat my mother so brutally was something I'll never be able to forget. He broke her arm multiple times, pulled chunks of hair from her head, and even when she had seizures, he would just let her lie there on the floor as if he didn't care whether she lived or died. I was the one who would rush to her side, trying desperately to wake her up, to make sure she was okay.

The fear that consumed me during those moments was overwhelming, a fear that never really went away. I begged my mother to stop provoking him, to just be quiet, to do whatever it took to keep him calm, but it never worked. She would yell back, refusing to be silenced, and the violence would escalate.

It's hard to describe the toll that all of this took on me. Growing up in such a toxic environment, where violence and fear were everyday occurrences, shaped me in ways I'm still trying to understand. It's left scars that will never fully heal, memories that will always haunt me. But it's also made me stronger in some ways. I've had to learn how to cope, how to survive, and how to find some semblance of peace in the midst of chaos. But the trauma of those years is something that will always be a part of me, no matter how much time passes.

The depth of my hatred for my father is something I never truly understood until I was much older. It wasn't just anger or frustration; it was a deep, burning hatred that consumed me. I hated life, and I hated God. For a long time, I couldn't even bring myself to believe in God because how could a God allow all of this to happen? How could I have been born into a family so filled with violence, with a father who didn't seem capable of love, not even for his own family?

Every time I locked myself in the bathroom, it wasn't just to escape the chaos outside, it was to try to find some way to cope with the chaos inside me. I started hurting myself because I didn't know what else to do. I felt so much pain, so much confusion, and there was no one I could turn to, no one who could understand what I was going through.

I would hit my face and scratch it until I looked like a joke, like something out of a nightmare. I would cut my face until it bled, hoping that the physical pain would drown out the emotional pain. But when that wasn't enough, when I couldn't feel that type of physical pain anymore, I started banging my head against the bathroom wall. I would do it over and over until blood streamed down my face. The sight of my own blood became almost comforting in a sick way because it was proof that I was still alive, that I could still feel something, even if it was just pain.

I didn't know how to deal with any of what was happening to me, around me, or inside my mind. I was too young, too scared, and too ashamed to ask for help. I couldn't call the cops because the shame of what the rest of my family would think was unbearable. I didn't want anyone to know what was going on inside our home. I didn't want to ruin my parents' name, even though they were the ones causing all the pain. Every time I reached out to someone, it was in a whisper, hidden in the secrecy of the bathroom. I would tell whoever would listen that I needed help, that I couldn't take it anymore, but the advice was always the same: "Pack your things and leave." As if it was that simple.

But it wasn't simple. I couldn't leave because leaving meant abandoning my mother, and I couldn't bear the thought of leaving her behind, defenseless and alone with my father. I knew if I left, my mom would be in even greater danger. So, I stayed. I sacrificed my own happiness, my safety, my sanity, my own life, just to make sure she would be okay. I begged my mom to leave with me so many times, but she always refused. She said it would bring shame onto our family, and that it would ruin our reputation. She didn't want to leave my father with nothing, even though he deserved nothing after everything he had done.

The weight of that decision to stay to protect my mother, was unbearable at times. I felt like I was trapped in a nightmare with no way out. The abhorrence I had for my father only grew stronger with each passing day, and it began to seep into every part of my life like a thick poison. It colored every interaction I had because, through the lens of my childhood, I had learned not to trust anyone, and I didn't let anyone get close to me because I was so terrified of being hurt again. I didn't see any way out of the darkness that surrounded me, and I didn't know how to ask for help. I was alone in my pain, and it felt like it was going to consume me completely.

Looking back, I realize that staying was the only choice I felt I had, but the sacrifice came at a huge cost. It took years for me to even begin to heal from the trauma of those days, and there are still parts of me that are scarred and will never fully recover. However, I also realize that in some ways, that pain made me stronger. It taught me how to survive, how to protect myself and the people I love. It taught me that even in the darkest times, there's still a part of me that won't give up that will keep fighting no matter what. It's a strength born out of pain, and it's a strength that came at a price.

My father never cared about where we were when he would lose his temper and start beating my mom and me. I remember one of our family members had a big party at their house one evening—a joyous occasion that felt like a world away from the turmoil inside our family. The house was filled with laughter, the clinking of glasses, and the aroma of freshly cooked food wafting through the air. I was upstairs hanging out with the other kids, trying to distract myself from the anxiety that always loomed over me.

But then, I heard it, a piercing scream that cut through the noise of the party like a knife. My heart dropped as I rushed to the window, my hands trembling as I pushed aside the curtain. I saw my mom outside, and the sight made my blood run cold. My dad was beating her in front of everyone. His hands moved with a rage I had seen too many times before, but this time, it was different. This time, it was public. My mom's cries echoed in my ears, her face contorted in pain as she tried to shield herself from his blows. Blood trickled down her face, and I could see her arm hanging at an unnatural angle, broken in two different places. I felt frozen, like my feet were cemented to the ground. I wanted to run down and help her, but I was paralyzed with fear. What shocked me even more was the reaction—or rather, the lack of it—from everyone around. People just stood there, watching as if it was a normal occurrence, as if my mother's suffering was just another part of the evening's entertainment. I felt a mix of anger, shame, and helplessness wash over me. How could they just stand there and do nothing? Why wasn't anyone stepping in to help her? It was as if her pain was invisible to them, or worse, irrelevant.

That night, after what felt like an eternity, my mom left. She went to stay with her sister-in-law, a place she hoped would offer some safety. My dad, of course, wasn't going to let that slide. The next day, he went to retrieve her, but her relatives didn't allow her to leave. I was left behind, alone with my dad. The silence in the house was ominous, filled only with the echoes of the violence I had witnessed.

I remember crying, begging my mom to take me with her, to not leave me alone with him. I clung to her, desperate for the safety and comfort only she could provide, but my dad ripped me away, dragging me by my hair back into the house. He was seething, his eyes filled with a hatred I couldn't understand. He told me I wasn't allowed to see my mom anymore, and at that moment, I felt a deep, piercing hatred for him. I was just a child, desperate for my mother, but I knew I had to keep quiet. I knew that if I fought back if I showed any resistance, it would only make things worse for her.

For almost a week, I didn't see my mom. I had no way of contacting her, no idea if she was okay. I felt abandoned, left in the clutches of a man who seemed to have nothing but contempt for me. I cried myself to sleep every night, praying that she would come back, that this nightmare would end. When she finally returned, I felt a mix of relief and dread. She told my dad that when he was ready to talk, she would be waiting. But there was no warmth, no reconciliation—just cold, hard resolve. My dad took me to Starbucks that day, of all places, and sat me down for a conversation I wasn't prepared for. He told me he wanted to divorce my mom, that it was over. I remember feeling a cold sweat break out across my skin as I realized what that meant. I told him to go ahead and leave her, but that I would be living with my mom. His response was cold, final. "That's not an option," he said. "You'll have to live with me."

I felt a wave of panic rise in my chest. The thought of living alone with my father, without my mom to protect me, was unbearable. I knew that if they divorced, I wouldn't survive it. I would rather die than live with him by myself. I went home and begged my mom not to let my dad divorce her, to please make it work. I was just a kid, scared out of my mind, thinking only of my own fear and not realizing the immense burden I was placing on her. I was selfish, desperate to keep her close, even if it meant she had to suffer more.

The situation at home only worsened. My parents stopped sleeping in the same room, the tension between them growing thicker with each passing day. Every night, I would wake up in a cold sweat, terrified that something had happened to my mom. I would tiptoe to her room, gently waking her and asking her to come to sleep in my bed. I would hold her tight, trying to protect her in the only way I knew how. I could feel her pain, her despair, and it broke my heart. This wasn't what marriage was supposed to be like. This wasn't the life I wanted for her or for myself.

For a long time, I didn't believe in marriage. I couldn't. How could I, after seeing what it had done to my mom? I didn't want to end up like her, trapped in a loveless, violent relationship, unable to escape because of fear or societal pressure. I didn't want a man like my father, and I didn't want to spend my life unhappy, living in constant fear.

Chapter: 27
Understanding Me, Del, Dad, and Fish

When Del was alive, she would cook something new every single day for my grandfather. I mean, breakfast, lunch, and dinner were never repeated, she always managed to whip up something fresh and exciting. She was undeniably one of the best cooks in our family, a culinary magician who seemed to have an endless repertoire of recipes. One day, she decided to cook fish for my grandfather. Now, my grandparents kept their frozen food in the garage in a big, old-fashioned freezer. I was curious and insisted on going with her, but she told me to stay inside and not to come out. Being a stubborn child, I didn't listen and followed her into the garage anyway.

The garage was dark and freezing cold, with that eerie quiet that only a rarely used space can have. I thought it would be funny to scare Del, so I stayed close behind her, ready to shout "Boo!" as soon as she opened the freezer. But as soon as the lid of the freezer was lifted and the overhead light flickered on, I wasn't the one doing the scaring; instead, I was the one being scared. The sight that greeted me was a massive fish, frozen solid, with its lifeless eyes staring straight at me. It felt as though the fish was accusing me of something, its cold, unblinking gaze cutting through the dim light. I was so terrified that I screamed, with tears welling up in my eyes, and bolted back into the house as fast as my little legs could carry me.

Shaking with fear, I asked Del why the fish had eyes and why it was staring at me like that. She explained matter-of-factly that the fish was dead, and she needed to cut it up and clean it for lunch. That was the moment my deep-seated aversion to fish was born. From that day on, I couldn't stand the thought of eating fish. The image of that frozen fish with its haunting eyes burned itself into my memory, and every time I even thought about the fish, I could see it staring back at me.

As I grew older, my distaste for fish only intensified, much to my father's dismay. He loved fish and couldn't understand why I didn't share his enthusiasm. No matter how many times I told him I hated fish, he refused to accept it. He would go off on me if I didn't eat what he made, insisting that I needed to learn to appreciate it. One night, when I was about seven or eight years old, my dad decided to make fish for dinner. He sat down at the table with me and insisted on feeding it to me himself, determined to make me eat it whether I liked it or not.

But I couldn't swallow it. I just couldn't. I kept the fish in my mouth, refusing to chew, my cheeks puffed out like a chipmunk hoarding nuts, tears streaming down my face as my dad yelled at me to swallow. He couldn't understand why I was so resistant, and the more he yelled, the more stubborn I became. Finally, he gave up in frustration and left the table. The moment he was out of sight, I spit all of the fish out into my napkin, my body trembling with relief.

Even now, at 29 years old, I still don't care for fish or seafood. The thought of it brings back that childhood memory of the fish with its cold, dead eyes. However, I've learned to tolerate it in social situations. If I'm out with friends and they drag me to a sushi restaurant, I'll force myself to take a small bite of something, trying not to let my disgust show. Sushi, to me, is like a confusing wonder in my mouth, an explosion of flavors and textures that I can't quite make sense of. Every bite feels like a challenge, and I always have a glass of water ready to chug right after, just to get it down. Though I've made some progress in overcoming my aversion, that childhood trauma still lingers. I think it always will.

Chapter: 28
Understanding My Parents

As I've mentioned before, my parents were struggling hard financially. It got so bad that we almost lost our home three times, and it kept going up for foreclosure. My father took out numerous loans and even filed for bankruptcy twice just to save our home. The stress was beyond overwhelming, and I kept telling them that we should sell the house while we could and rent an apartment. But my parents couldn't agree to that idea. They were so deeply attached to the house, and I understood why. It was our first home, something they had worked so hard to finally own. But the stress and constant headaches were not worth it.

Their struggles were taking a toll on me, too. I began to feel physically sick from the anxiety of it all. I would literally drive around for hours just to avoid going home and dealing with their stress. Even when I had no gas left, I would park my car somewhere and sleep for a couple of hours until I felt ready to face the reality waiting for me at home.

It reached a point where my parents couldn't even pay the electricity bill, and we lived without water or power for almost a month and a half. They owed about $8,000, and the Department of Water and Power (DWP) demanded the full amount, or at least half, before they would restore our services. It was money we simply didn't have, and we didn't know where to turn for help.

I cried so much during that time because I finally knew what it was like to truly struggle. I felt the weight of that struggle deeply, and I finally understood what it must feel like to be homeless. My mom would boil water and fill buckets so I could take a semblance of a shower every day.

Every night, she would light candles around the house. We would sit together in the dark, eating dinner, not knowing what the next day would bring.

Sometimes, to escape, I would go to the gym or visit a friend's house just to have food and take a hot shower. Every time I stood under that hot water at my friend's place, I would cry in silence. I would press my forehead against the cold tiles, and I would beg God to stop all the tests, to give my family and me a break because we couldn't take much more.

Then, the day finally came when we were able to pay the bill and get our water and power back. I remember feeling like I was at Disneyland, the happiest kid alive. The first time I flipped a light switch and the room flooded with light, I felt a wave of relief wash over me. It was such a simple thing, something I had taken for granted my entire life, but in that moment, it meant everything.

Knowing I could finally take a hot shower, that my mom wouldn't need to boil gallons of water or fill buckets anymore, it was the best feeling in the world.

When my parents finally agreed to sell our home after years of ongoing arguments and desperate attempts to save it, I felt an overwhelming sense of relief. It was as if a heavy weight was finally being lifted off our shoulders. I thought, maybe, just maybe, my parents would finally find some peace and happiness now that their biggest source of stress would be behind them.

We ended up renting a small house about 15 minutes away from our old home. The change was immediate and almost magical. I remember loving the new place from the moment we moved in. For the first time in years, I actually enjoyed coming home. It was such a stark contrast to how I used to feel, constantly dreading the tension and conflict that awaited me at our old house.

My parents looked different too. They seemed lighter, almost as if they were rediscovering who they were without the crushing burden of financial stress weighing them down. They stopped fighting and became civil with each other, something I hadn't seen in what felt like forever. They were more relaxed, kinder to one another, and it created a warmth in our home that had been missing for so long.

This new dynamic between them was transformative for me as well. For the first time in my life, I actually wanted to be around them. I found myself wanting to spend time with them, to be part of this newfound peace. It was something I had never felt before. Seeing how something as significant as selling our home, a decision that had been so agonizing, could bring about such a positive change made me incredibly happy.

It was a reminder that sometimes, letting go of something, even when it's painful, can open the door to new possibilities and healing. The house we left behind was more than just a structure; it had become a symbol of all the stress, anger, and unhappiness that had plagued our family. But in letting it go, we were able to find a fresh start and with it, a chance to rebuild our relationships and find some peace.

A year passed in our new home, and just when I thought we had finally found some stability, we got a call from our landlord. Our lease was ending, and we were given until August to find a new place. The news hit me hard, but it was the look on my parents' faces that alarmed me the most. I could see them spiraling out of control, the familiar signs of stress taking over. The drinking started again, and with it came the fighting, an all-too-familiar cycle I had hoped we'd left behind.

I tried to reassure them, telling them not to stress, that we would find a new place to live, but deep down, I knew this situation was different. My parents didn't want to rent anymore; they wanted to buy a home again. That scared me because I wasn't sure if they could afford it. I knew the financial strain that buying a house would put on them, and I feared we might end up right back where we started, with all the anxiety and tension that came with it.

I realized, though, that this was a decision they had to make on their own. I had supported my family for many years, both emotionally and financially, but I was reaching a point where I couldn't do it anymore. I had to be a bit selfish and start taking care of my own life. I couldn't keep carrying the weight of their decisions indefinitely, especially knowing that sooner or later, I would need to focus on building a life for myself, getting married, having a family, and supporting them in whatever way I could. Despite my concerns, I tried to help them as much as I could, offering advice and looking at potential options, but I knew my limits. The reality was that I needed to start setting boundaries and making sure I was taking care of myself too. I was ready to step back a bit, to let my parents take the reins of their own lives, and to start focusing on my own path forward. It was a scary thought, but I knew it was necessary for all of us to grow and find peace.

As a family, we hadn't decided yet what to do, whether to buy a new house or find another place to rent—but I knew that whatever happened in the future, it would have to be for the better. I hoped that we could find a solution that wouldn't plunge us back into the chaos we had worked so hard to escape.

Chapter: 29
Understanding How College Works

When I was in college, I struggled a lot. I wasn't the smartest kid, but I had a genuine love for learning new things, especially when it came to subjects that fascinated me. The one subject I truly couldn't stand was math. I hated it with a passion, and to this day, that feeling hasn't changed. I never understood why we needed to learn algebra—who in their right mind ever uses it in real life? It felt like a pointless exercise, a frustration that never seemed to end. Every math class felt like a battle, and no matter how hard I tried, I just couldn't wrap my head around the concepts. It was like hitting a brick wall over and over again.

But while math was my nemesis, my major in college was my absolute love, criminal justice. I was madly in love with it from the moment I took my first class. There was something about understanding the psychology behind criminal behavior, the why and how of it all, that just pulled me in. I was captivated by the idea of learning how criminals' minds work, what drives them to commit such insane acts, and how society could hold them accountable. My dream career was to become a criminal judge, someone who could not only interpret the law but also understand the deeper motivations behind criminal actions.

I threw myself into my studies with everything I had. I took every course related to criminal justice that I could find. I was like a sponge, soaking up all the knowledge and insights my professors had to offer. One of the most thrilling experiences I had was when I got the chance to go to a juvenile hall to interview some of the kids who were incarcerated there, aged 12-17 years old. I was scared at first, terrified, actually, but I loved the rush. There was something so raw and real about hearing their stories, understanding their backgrounds, and seeing the stark reality of where their choices had led them. Some of these kids were in jail for committing theft, others for assaults, and I even got to interview one child who was there for attempted murder. Each story was a piece of a puzzle that I was trying to understand.

For me, at the time, school was going great. I saw my whole life plan laid out in front of me, and I was so excited about the possibilities. I imagined myself going to law school, excelling, and eventually sitting on the bench as a criminal judge, making decisions that would impact lives and, hopefully, make a difference in the world. It all seemed so clear, so within reach.

But then my dad came back from Afghanistan, and everything changed. He had other plans for me, and those plans didn't include becoming a criminal judge. He didn't see the value in my passion for criminal justice. Instead, he persuaded me, no, pressured me, to change my major to something he deemed more respectable, more practical, like dental or any type of doctor. I was crushed. I had spent so much time and energy pursuing what I loved, only to be told that it wasn't good enough, that it wasn't the right path.

I hated the medical field. I had worked in it for a while, and I knew it wasn't for me. I hated everything about it, the smell of antiseptic, the cold, sterile environments, the pressure of dealing with life and death situations. I loved helping people, but I couldn't stand the sight of blood. The thought of someone bleeding out on me was enough to make me feel sick. Honestly, the medical field just sounded so boring to me. It was the opposite of what I wanted to do with my life, but my dad was insistent, and eventually, I gave in. I changed my major to dental, but I hated it so much that I barely showed up to class. I was almost failing all my classes because my heart just wasn't in it.

At the same time, my parents were struggling financially, and they really needed my help. The weight of responsibility was crushing me. I felt like I was drowning, trying to keep up with school and work, but nothing was going right. Eventually, it got to the point where I had to drop out of school without telling them. I started working three jobs just to help out at home. It was grueling. I was working around the clock, and the stress was unbearable. The worst part was that the house mortgage was on me. I had to pay at least half, and at that time, our house payment was almost $5k a month. As a college student with student loans and personal bills piling up, I was barely keeping my head above water.

I felt like my dreams were slipping away from me. Every day, I went to work instead of class, watching as the future I had imagined slowly faded into the distance. It was heartbreaking. I had been so excited to go to law school to accomplish everything I had dreamed of, but instead, I found myself trapped in a life I didn't want, carrying a burden that was too heavy to bear. My passion for criminal justice, for understanding and making a difference, was still there, but I had to bury it under the weight of financial obligations and family expectations. It was one of the hardest, most soul-crushing experiences of my life.

You can say that the strictest parents make the sneakiest kids, and I was no exception. I hated lying to my parents, but in my mind, I had no choice. They had pushed me to the point where everything in my life was almost a lie. I lied so much growing up to my parents that it became second nature, but I never lied to those around me, my cousins, my friends. With them, I was always honest because I hated the feeling of deceit, and I never felt the need to lie to people who accepted me for who I was. My parents were a different story altogether. I had no freedom, no life of my own; I couldn't breathe when I was with them. They were constantly interrogating me, never allowing me to do anything or to be who I truly was. It was suffocating, and I was young and stupid, desperate to escape that prison they had built around me.

When graduation time came around, I knew I was in deep trouble. The lies I had spun over the years were about to catch up with me, and I was terrified. But instead of coming clean, I did something even more foolish. My friends and I came up with the scariest, most outlandish graduation plan, and to be honest, I never thought I could actually pull it off. I knew this idea was going to get me caught, and it would be way worse than just telling my parents the truth. But I was determined to see it through. I was in too deep, and the fear of my parents' reaction drove me to do something reckless.

The day before the graduation ceremony, I went to UCLA with my friend Jake. He was always the ride-or-die type, willing to do whatever it took to help me, and this time was no different. We needed graduation tickets, and the pressure was on. Jake paid $300 to get me two tickets, which was absurd because the tickets were only $5 each. But Jake wasn't taking any chances; he wanted to make sure we secured them, so we went around the entire campus asking students for extra tickets. We ended up with three, and though it was a crazy plan, I loved him for it. Life eventually took us in different directions, and we don't talk as often anymore, but I will never forget what he did for me that day.

With the tickets in hand, we headed to the student store, where I executed the next part of my plan. I walked in and confidently told them that my cousin had originally decided not to attend the graduation but had changed her mind at the last minute, asking me to pick up her cap and gown. It was a bold lie, but to my shock, they didn't even check for her name or information; they just handed me a package that said UCLA Class of 2022 with the cap and gown inside. I couldn't believe how easy it was.

That night, I couldn't sleep. My heart was pounding in my chest, and I was beyond scared. I knew deep down that this plan wouldn't work. How was I supposed to walk down that stage, pretending to be a graduate, and not have my name called during the ceremony? The more I thought about it, the more I realized how insane this idea was. But I was in too deep, and there was no turning back now.

It was the day of my big "graduation," and the whole day, I was a bundle of nerves. My heart was pounding so hard I thought it might burst out of my chest. I could see my mom was genuinely excited, while my dad wore his usual blank expression, betraying nothing of what he was thinking. The entire morning, I was desperately trying to figure out a way to get out of going to the ceremony. I didn't want to hurt them, but I also wanted this nightmare of lies to be over. In a moment of panic, I decided to do something drastic. I went into the kitchen and grabbed a bag of dried mulberries and walnuts, the one thing I'm deathly allergic to. I ate the whole bag, hoping, praying, that something would happen to me. I wanted an allergic reaction to hit so hard that I'd be rushed to the hospital, giving me an out from this unbearable situation. But nothing happened. I sat there, waiting for the familiar tightening of my throat, the swelling, the panic, but nothing. I couldn't understand why I wasn't dying. It was as if God was telling me, "You better get this graduation in order because you are not dying today."

With no allergic reaction to save me, I had no choice but to follow through with the plan. We got ready, and as we headed to UCLA for the big graduation, I felt like I was walking to my execution. Jake, my ever-loyal friend, came along for moral support, and my girl Kelly was there too, ready to help the plan go off without a hitch. My parents dropped me off so they could park the car, and I immediately started walking to the other side of the campus to meet up with Kelly. The moment I got into her car, we drove a few blocks away to Habibi Cafe, a spot we used to frequent. Kelly ordered us some food and hookah, hoping it would calm me down, but I couldn't eat or smoke. My nerves were shot, and all I could think about was how this could all blow up in my face.

We had Jake keeping us posted on the graduation ceremony. He was there, sitting across from my parents, keeping an eye on them and texting me updates. Meanwhile, I was glued to my phone, watching the ceremony live-streamed, feeling like a fraud with every passing minute. My parents kept blowing up my phone, texting and calling, asking where I was because they couldn't see me. To make matters worse, I had completely forgotten that they handed out handbooks with the names of all the students who were graduating, and of course, my name wasn't in it. Jake noticed this and immediately alerted me. My heart sank further, but I kept declining their calls, too terrified to answer and not sure what to say.

Three agonizing hours later, the graduation finally ended. Kelly and I drove back to campus, and somehow, I managed to find the doors where all the graduates were exiting. As soon as I got there, I slipped into the crowd of students walking out, blending in like I belonged. I spotted my parents waiting, searching the crowd for me. Kelly, being the best wingwoman ever, greeted me with flowers and balloons, congratulating me in front of my parents like it was all legit. My dad's face was a mix of confusion and anger, and I was bracing myself, ready for the explosion. But Kelly, ever the quick thinker, jumped in and suggested, "Let's take a family photo," diffusing the tension for a moment.

After the photos, as we were walking away, my dad asked the dreaded question, "Why wasn't your name in the book?" My mind raced for a plausible excuse, and I immediately replied, "You had to pay extra to have your name in there, and I didn't think it was worth it." It was a weak lie, but it was the best I could come up with on the spot.

We went out to dinner afterward, and Jake texted me, asking if everything was okay. I replied, "I think we pulled it off." My mom was still on cloud nine, oblivious to the truth, but I could tell my dad wasn't entirely convinced. There was a tension in the air, a lingering doubt in his eyes. But I kept my cool, playing the role of the dutiful daughter who had just graduated from UCLA, all the while knowing that I had narrowly escaped a disaster, at least for the moment.

Now, you're probably wondering how I managed to get away with showing a bachelor's degree when I never actually graduated. It sounds insane, but I bought it online and had someone custom-make it for me. It's crazy what you can find on the internet when you're desperate. The fake degree looked so real that even I almost believed it myself. But after everything died down and the dust settled, I was left with an overwhelming sense of guilt. I couldn't sleep for weeks, haunted by the lies I had woven and the fact that I had deceived my parents on something so monumental.

The guilt still lingers, and there are moments when I wish I had just come clean. But at that time, the fear of disappointing my parents, especially my dad, outweighed everything else. I'm incredibly grateful to the people around me who knew what was happening and supported me through it all. They understood the impossible situation I was in, and I can't imagine pulling it off without their help. They were my team, my safety net, and I don't think I would have been able to do it on my own.

Even though I pulled off the charade, a part of me always wanted to go back to school and finish my degree for real, just for myself. But as I got older, I came to realize that you don't necessarily need a degree to be successful. You can achieve great things if you're determined and willing to work hard. I've faced so many struggles, failed countless times, but I'm not giving up. I know that I will eventually make it and find success on my own terms.

Chapter: 30
Understanding The Freedom of Traveling

It was about two years ago when my dad's little sister was getting remarried in Paris, and I thought to myself, "What a great excuse to get out of not only my house but also to finally see what's outside of America!" I struggled so much trying to buy a plane ticket; it was about $1,700 for a round trip at the time. I remember I didn't book my flight until three days before leaving, and I had no money left. I didn't know how I was going to survive this trip, but I knew one way or another I was leaving, and no one was going to stop me.

I got on the flight, and at first, I was beyond excited and so happy. Of course, I was a bit nervous because I was worried about my money situation. I hadn't seen my dad's side of the family since I was about eight years old. That was over 12 years ago. I had no idea what my cousins looked like or how they would even recognize me when they were picking me up from the airport.

After a long 14-hour nonstop flight, big mistake, I finally landed in Paris, the city of love. First things first: Paris is not what it seems. People are rude, the city is dirty, and, honestly, it felt like Los Angeles but 10 times busier. I got to the airport in France, and of course, everything was delayed. I waited over an hour for my luggage, and I was beyond nervous because I had no idea who was picking me up from the airport.

When I finally left the airport, I saw a man just staring at me and smiling, and it was crazy—I instantly knew that it was my little cousin, Alex. It was insane; I had no idea he even knew how to speak English, but, damn, his English was better than mine! Of course, he had a French accent, but it was so cool to me to know that I had family in Europe. My little French family.

We got in the car, and he told me it was his birthday today, and they were having a party at his mom's house. Mind you, it was 10 pm when I left the airport, and I looked disgusting. So, I asked Alex if he could take me to my hotel so I could freshen up and go to the party.

10 pm in Paris during the summer is when the sun starts to set. It was probably the most beautiful sunset I had ever seen. It looked like something that came out of a fairy tale movie. When I finally got to my aunt's house, it was close to midnight, and I was super jet-lagged, I mean, wired up, thinking I was still in the LA time zone jet lagged.

I walked into the house, and I immediately felt the love from my entire family. I was welcomed with open arms, and the best part was that my LA family was there as well. The cousins that I grew up with back home were there, and I felt at home. I didn't know how I would feel in a foreign country with people I didn't really know, but I felt embraced and accepted right away.

We celebrated Alex's birthday, and then it was time for my older cousin and me to go back to our hotel. Alex drove us, and we asked him to stay with us because it was late, and I didn't want my little cousin to drive back home alone. That night was one of the most memorable nights of my life. My two guy cousins and I bonded, which is something we had never done before.

It was about 2 am, and we couldn't sleep, so we decided to go outside to have some wine and smoke some weed to maybe help us go to sleep. By the way, it is illegal to smoke weed during the week in Paris. They would arrest you right away without hesitation. I'm also not a smoker, but at that point, I just really wanted to sleep and was down to try anything.

We sat outside under the soft glow of Parisian street lights, and for the first time, I felt like I was living the life I always imagined, free, unburdened, and connected with family in a way I had never been before. We talked about everything, from our childhoods to our dreams, and I realized how much I had missed out on growing up apart from them. It was one of those rare moments in life where everything felt right, where I felt truly alive and at peace.

This trip, despite the initial stress and challenges, became a turning point for me. It reminded me of the importance of family, of taking risks, and of finding joy in unexpected moments. Even though Paris wasn't the romanticized city I had envisioned, it gave me something far more valuable, a deeper connection with my roots and a renewed sense of belonging.

Two hours went by, and we were all wide awake, so my older cousin mentioned he had some sleeping pills and asked if we wanted some. Mind you, we were high, drunk, and jet-lagged, which means our brains were essentially on autopilot, lol. We took the pill, and an hour went by, but we were still wide awake. My older cousin said he had to go downstairs because he still had work to do, so he was going to do his Zoom call elsewhere in case we fell asleep.

Alex and I stayed up, telling stories and joking around, when we both conked out out of nowhere. We didn't remember anything after that. My check-out time from the hotel was 11 am, but I kept waking up thinking I was hearing the phone ring. I kept telling myself I was dreaming. It was 12 pm when the phone wouldn't stop ringing. I finally woke up and answered it. The hotel receptionist told me that if we didn't leave in the next 10 minutes, we would be charged for another night. Panic set in, and I started screaming, waking everyone up. I threw everything into my luggage, and we all rushed out of the hotel.

Mind you, I didn't go to the bathroom or even wash my face. I left the hotel in my pajamas with crazy morning hair. We jumped into Alex's car, and as soon as I got in, I fell back asleep. I was so heavily medicated that it didn't matter what my cousins were doing; I was out cold.

We had to meet the family in the city, and I was mortified at the thought of seeing everyone for the first time looking like a complete mess. We parked the car, and I swear, I felt like I was doing the walk of shame. It was way worse than that. I was dragging my luggage through the streets, begging my older cousin to get us into the hotel so we could change and get ready before facing everyone. But, of course, with my luck, that didn't happen. The hotel wouldn't let us into the room without my aunt because the reservations were under her name, and they were still an hour away.

So, I sat in the hotel lobby, noticing how everyone was staring at me. They definitely knew I was a tourist and a disheveled one at that! After what felt like an eternity, my family finally arrived at the hotel. Let's just say the first meet and greet wasn't exactly how I imagined it. My aunt was so happy to see me but couldn't help questioning my appearance. I had to explain the whole ordeal, and of course, everyone thought it was hilarious.

Finally, we got inside our rooms, and I wasn't prepared for what came next. My aunt had booked two rooms for 10 people with just one bed in each room. The parents got their own room while the cousins had to make do. Three people squeezed onto a queen bed; the eldest cousin slept on the floor next to the toilet, and the rest of us piled on top of each other in the living room, somehow making it work.

After we got ready, we all gathered at the hotel bar and made our way to a fancy restaurant, where we met the rest of the family. It was overwhelming, but in a good way, to see everyone all at once. However, as the night went on, I started to miss my parents. I know it sounds crazy, right? Here I was in Paris, surrounded by family, but seeing everyone with their loved ones made me long for my own parents. I wished they were there with me.

My time in Paris wasn't as great as I had hoped. I got super homesick and found myself crying almost every day for a week, wanting to go back home. Frankly, I hated Paris, and I wasn't enjoying my time there. Everyone was giving me a hard time, not letting me breathe or do anything on my own. My entire family had seen Paris so many times that they didn't care about sightseeing, and they wouldn't let me go alone either.

One of my biggest goals while in Paris was to visit my grandparents' graves and bring flowers. I had promised my dad I would do this and send him a picture. Unfortunately, when the day came for me to go, my aunts didn't allow it. They gave me some lame excuse about it being too far away and how they didn't have time. They made sure it was the day of the rehearsal dinner so they could use that as another excuse for me not to go.

I called my parents crying, telling them I wanted to come home. I cried so much that I got sick and nearly had to be taken to the hospital due to a high fever that came out of nowhere. After sleeping for 24 hours, I finally felt better, but I still missed home and my parents terribly. I missed my mom more than anything and just wanted to be with her. You're probably laughing at the idea of a grown adult crying for her mommy, but what can I say? I'm a mommy's girl.

Looking back, that trip to Paris was a mix of highs and lows. It was a lesson in understanding that sometimes reality doesn't match fantasy, and that's okay. It also made me appreciate my family and home even more, even if they drive me crazy sometimes.

It was finally the wedding day, and the atmosphere was charged with excitement and a bit of chaos as everyone was rushing to get ready. Somehow, I found myself doing everyone's makeup, even though I'm far from being a professional makeup artist. I guess my skills were decent enough because everyone seemed happy with the results. Once we were all ready, we headed to the venue, and I was blown away by how beautiful it was. The location was picture-perfect, right by the Eiffel Tower. The setting felt like something out of a dream, with the iconic structure looming majestically in the background as the sun set.

As I walked into the venue, I was taken aback by the simplicity of the outfits worn by the guests. In Europe, it seems, wedding attire can be quite understated. I saw a woman in jeans and boots, which was a stark contrast to my own outfit—I was wearing a full-length gown, something you might see at a gala. It made me feel a bit overdressed, but I quickly realized that the vibe was more laid-back than what I was used to at Middle Eastern weddings back home. Middle Easterners in Europe seem to embrace a more relaxed approach to celebrations, which was refreshing in its own way.

Despite the differences in style, the wedding itself was incredibly fun. It was probably one of the most enjoyable weddings I had attended in a long time. The joy in the air was palpable, and I was genuinely happy to see my aunt finding love again. What I didn't mention earlier is that her first husband, my uncle, passed away suddenly a few years back. This new marriage wasn't without its challenges, though. My cousins, her children, weren't exactly thrilled about their mother remarrying. I understood their feelings, as they might have felt like their mom was replacing their dad. But that wasn't the case at all.

My aunt had been alone after her children moved out, and it was only natural for her to want companionship. She deserved to have someone to share her life with, and her new husband seemed like a genuinely great guy. I could see how happy she was with him, and that made me happy too. Plus, I gained two new cousins through the marriage, as her husband had two young sons. It felt like our family was growing in a beautiful way, and the wedding was a celebration of that new beginning for all of us.

As I looked around at everyone dancing, laughing, and enjoying the night, I couldn't help but feel a deep sense of gratitude. This trip, despite its ups and downs, had brought me closer to my extended family, and it reminded me of the importance of love and connection, no matter how far apart we might be.

The wedding ended, and the next day, we all packed up and went our separate ways. For me, that meant heading to Switzerland to stay with my other aunt in Geneva, along with the rest of the family. Let me tell you, I fell head over heels in love with Geneva. It quickly became one of my favorite cities in the world. Everything about it—the food, the people, the serene beauty of the city—was simply amazing.

As soon as I arrived in Geneva, all the homesickness I had been feeling in Paris melted away. My aunt welcomed me with open arms, and she made sure I felt completely at home. It was like stepping into a different world, one where I was surrounded by warmth and love. I couldn't have asked for a better place to be.

Geneva wasn't just about reconnecting with family; it was also about indulging a little. I don't think I've ever shopped so much in my life. My aunt was incredibly generous, paying for everything during my stay. I never once had to pull out my wallet, which was a huge relief considering my financial situation. Of course, I tried to fake an offer to pay, even though I knew my card would probably decline, but it was the polite thing to do. I didn't want to come across as a freeloader, even though I knew my aunt wouldn't let me pay for anything.

I spent about four days in Geneva, soaking up every bit of the city's charm. It was a blissful escape from the stresses of everyday life, and I cherished every moment of it. But as much as I loved Geneva, I knew my time there was coming to an end. I had to leave and go visit my mom's side of the family in London. I was nervous but also excited. This was a family I knew well, having seen them many times throughout my life, so there was a certain comfort in that familiarity.

Saying goodbye to my European family in Geneva was hard. I hated the thought of leaving them behind, especially since I didn't know when I would see them again. I had grown so attached to them in such a short amount of time, and the thought of parting ways left a lump in my throat. I knew I was going to miss them a lot, but I also knew I had to continue my journey.

The day I was leaving for London, all hell broke loose. You know what they say: it's not a vacation without some type of drama. My mom's little brother decided to take matters into his own hands and act like he was my father. He called my parents after speaking to me, saying I shouldn't go to London because everyone in the family had COVID and I shouldn't be alone in a hotel. Mind you, I was 27 at the time. Who was he to call and tell me where I could and couldn't go? My mother called and said her brother had informed her that my London family didn't really want to see me and that it wasn't worth me going. My mom clearly believed her younger brother, which only fueled my frustration. But I didn't care, nor did I listen to anyone. I got on the flight and flew to London. I was tired of everyone telling me what I could and couldn't do. It's my life. Who is anyone to tell me how to live it? So what if people had COVID? I'm old enough to travel to a different country on my own and handle things myself.

When I landed in London, I wasn't in the best mood because of all the family drama. But then I saw a familiar goofy face at the airport: my amazing cousin Qais. He knew I wasn't in a great mood, so he decided to mess with me by letting me stress out at the airport trying to find him for 10 minutes while he was walking right behind me. When we finally got to the car, I let out all my anger, yelling at him for telling my uncle that his family had COVID and that I was staying at a hotel. I was so angry because it had caused so many problems for me. But Qais, being his usual calm and collected self, told me not to worry and to just say, "Fuck it," and enjoy my time in London since I was only there for three days.

Qais had reserved a hotel for me, and to my surprise, it was this beautiful little cottage up in the mountains. It was beyond beautiful, everything I could have asked for and more. It was my first time being alone in a hotel, and, not going to lie, I was a bit scared. I had these wild thoughts that some creep was going to come and murder me or that someone would stalk me to my room. I left all the lights on and the TV playing so anyone passing by would think whoever was inside was awake. I don't even think I slept for more than an hour at a time because I kept waking up thinking someone was in my room.

Chapter: 31
Eid in London

The next morning, I got up, ready to start my day, but I couldn't figure out how to turn the shower on. It got so frustrating that I had to call the front desk for help. When someone came and showed me how to turn the shower on, I felt ridiculous. All I had to do was turn the handle up and pull it out. After finally getting ready, I was pretty excited to go out and see London, especially since I found out that my cousins from Los Angeles were also in town and wanted to meet up. It was nice having my LA family with me; it felt like home in a different country.

London was nice, but honestly, it wasn't all that I had imagined. The weather is completely bipolar, so believe people when they tell you that. One minute it's hot, like tank-top-and-shorts hot, and the next minute it's cold and pouring rain. I had no idea how to dress, and my hair was a mess—frizzy and out of control like a poodle with an afro. Despite the weather, I managed to see all of London in one day. And let me just say the Queen's palace is not all that. I don't understand why people get so excited about it. There really isn't much to see or do; people just stand around and take pictures by the gate. In my opinion, it was super boring.

I've never walked so much in my life, almost 12 hours without a break, but I love walking, so I didn't even feel tired. When the day finally ended, Qais and I decided to check out some hookah lounges. Let me tell you, London has some great hookah lounges. It was my last day before I had to fly back home, and I wasn't too happy about leaving because I was having so much fun.

It was also Eid, a Muslim holiday, and it felt strange not celebrating with my entire family. But my London family made sure I wasn't getting homesick. They threw a lavish party, and it was incredible to see everyone again. I hadn't seen most of these people for over 10 years, yet they all knew who I was. We danced the night away, celebrating Eid. The streets were filled with colors, and fireworks lit up the sky. No one in LA celebrates Eid like the people in London. It was honestly one of the best experiences I've had.

The day of my return trip dawned, and while I knew my mom was excited to see me, I wasn't feeling the same way about returning. It was the longest I had been away from her, and I missed her terribly. But when it came to my dad, I didn't share the same enthusiasm. He's always been cold, distant, and devoid of emotions, so I doubted he even missed me while I was gone.

When I landed back home, I saw my parents waiting for me. My mom ran out of the car and gave me the biggest hug, and it felt so good to be wrapped in the warmth of her arms again.

When it was time to greet my dad, it was just a cold hello. Instead of a hug or any sign that he missed me and was glad I was back, he immediately started complaining about why my suitcase was so heavy. I was so annoyed. Why couldn't he just hug me and say, "I missed you," or "Welcome home," or something? It was like he didn't even care that I had been gone for so long.

When I got home, the feeling of being back was bittersweet. Sure, it was nice to be in my own space again, but the energy in the house was so negative and draining from the moment I walked in. I simply hated it. I never liked being home. I quickly went to unpack and decided that it was time to sleep because the jet lag coming back home was no joke. I ended up sleeping for four days straight, all day long. My parents didn't understand why I was sleeping so much and kept complaining that jet lag couldn't be that bad. I was so frustrated. I kept thinking, hello, you guys haven't traveled much since you came to America, and that was over 40 years ago.

In that moment, I made a promise to myself that from that day forward, I was going to take a mini vacation every month, even if it was just for a weekend. And every summer, I would start traveling around the world. I needed that escape from the toxic environment at home, and I was determined to keep that promise to myself. Even when I didn't go anywhere far, I would just stay with friends or by myself. I'd get a hotel for the weekend, run from the noise, and just relax.

Whenever my friends joined me, those weekends turned into the best times, with no one sleeping because we'd be out all night having fun. To keep my parents off my back, I'd simply tell them that I was going on work trips. It was hands down the best excuse, and it worked every time.

Those getaways became my sanctuary, a way to reclaim my peace and keep my sanity intact.

Chapter: 32
Understanding Therapy

Starting therapy three years ago was a turning point for me, though it wasn't easy to take that first step. The idea of opening up to a complete stranger about all the things I had been through, all the struggles I was facing, was terrifying. I was hesitant, even scared, but deep down, I knew I needed help. I could see that I was heading down a dangerous path, one that looked all too familiar. I was drinking more than I should, getting drunk almost every weekend, and it was starting to remind me of my parents' struggles with alcohol. The one thing I was proud of was that I recognized I had a problem. I just didn't know how to stop drinking. I didn't know how to help myself.

That's when I decided that I couldn't keep bottling everything up. I needed to talk to someone. My first therapy session was overwhelming. I spent the entire hour venting and crying, and when it was over, I thought, "This is pointless." It felt like all I was doing was talking in circles while someone listened and asked questions. I wanted to give up right then and there, to say, "Screw it," and just keep going the way I had been. But something inside me told me to keep going, to stick with it.

As time went on, I realized my therapist was different from what I expected. She didn't just listen; she actively worked with me. At the end of each session, she gave me assignments to do, practical steps to take in my daily life. She wasn't just someone who sat there and nodded while I talked. She was truly helping me work through my issues, and for the first time, I felt like I was getting somewhere.

I began to notice changes in myself. I was becoming more patient and calm, not just with other people but with myself. The anger that had always been simmering under the surface started to fade, and incredibly, I even stopped drinking for a while. I learned how to handle my liquor without getting sloppy, without making a fool of myself, but more importantly, without needing to numb myself from life.

Before therapy, when I drank, I was a fun drinker—at least at first. I'd laugh, I'd dance, I'd have a good time, but if someone made me mad, I'd turn into a completely different person. I became verbally abusive, seeing nothing but red. I felt like I was always right, and everyone else was wrong. Therapy helped me recognize that side of myself and taught me how to control it.

I continued therapy for about a year, and I applied everything I learned to my daily life. Even after I stopped going to therapy, I never forgot what I had learned. I still apply those lessons today. For example, when someone pisses me off or says something negative about me, I allow it to pass without reacting. I don't snap, I don't cuss people out. Instead, I sit back quietly and let them do their thing. I've learned that I don't need to lower myself to their level of negativity. I know that people like that aren't worth my time or energy.

Therapy taught me to stay away from negativity and those who bring me down. I've learned that you can't please everyone in life. Some people will love you and accept you for who you are, while others will try to bring you down. You have to learn to navigate away from those who are bad for your energy. The people you allow into your life are a reflection of you. If the people around you are always negative, you will be too. So, I do my best to keep positive people around me. Their energy lifts me up, and I feel better for it.

Of course, life happens, and everyone has their ups and downs. That's normal, and I try to be there for people when they need someone to talk to. I've also learned that my mental health is more important. When I start to feel overwhelmed, I know it's okay to distance myself for my own sanity. I've learned how to take care of myself, and that's something I'm proud of.

Chapter: 33
Understanding Myself

Imagine the emotional rollercoaster you went through during your teenage years. Being 17 is hard enough, but then imagine having to face the loss of your grandmother and then nearly lose your mother right after that. It would have been absolutely devastating. The overwhelming grief and confusion, coupled with the feeling of abandonment, would have made life feel unbearable. It's understandable that you would have felt so much anger and despair, especially when it seemed like life was taking away everyone you loved. Especially if your mom fell into a coma, it would have felt like the final straw, stacked on top of your father not being there. It's as if you were left completely alone, being so young, and no one should have to bear that kind of weight. The fear of becoming an orphan, the fear of losing the last person you had, would have made every day feel like a struggle just to survive.

And then, when your mom finally woke up but didn't remember you, it would have felt like the cruelest twist of fate. To see her alive and looking at you but not recognize you, her own daughter, would have been heartbreaking beyond words. I know how lost and helpless you would have felt, trying to remind her of who you were, trying to hold on to the hope that she would remember.

That day when your uncle picked you up from school would have been filled with so many mixed emotions. You didn't care about any surprises; all you wanted was to be with your mom, to see her and make sure she was okay. When you walked into his house and saw her lying on the couch, asking you for a hug because she missed her daughter, it would have felt like a miracle. All the pain, all the despair you had been carrying, would have lifted in that moment. Hugging her so hard, feeling her arms around you, would have been the most comforting and loving moment you had experienced in a long time.

That day was a reminder that even in the darkest times, there can be moments of light. It was a moment that brought you back to life, that gave you hope, and reminded you of the love that still existed, even when everything else seemed to be falling apart. It's these moments that help us push through the pain and find the strength to keep going.

Depression is a silent struggle, often hidden behind a smile or a laugh. On the outside, people may assume I have this perfect life, that everything is smooth sailing because they see a well-put-together facade. They don't see the internal battle I fight every single day just to get out of bed. People assume that because I come from a Middle Eastern family with cultural expectations and community standards, I must be fine. They think I have no reason to be depressed, that I should be grateful for what I have. What they don't realize is that depression doesn't discriminate based on background, wealth, or status.

For Middle Eastern parents, mental health is often an alien concept. When I first tried to explain to my parents that I was struggling with depression, their reactions were a mix of confusion and disbelief. They couldn't fathom what could possibly be wrong. "What stress could you have?" they asked as if depression only happens to people with visible hardships. They didn't understand that despite the material comfort, I was battling a darkness that consumed me from the inside.

I tried to explain that it wasn't about the external factors; it was about the internal turmoil that I couldn't control. The overwhelming sadness, the feeling of worthlessness, and the constant questioning of my purpose in life. But they didn't get it. They looked at me as if I was speaking a foreign language, as if depression was something that could be willed away with a little more positivity or gratitude.

Every day, I wake up and tell myself that I have to make it through. That no matter what the day brings, I have to keep going. Some days, it's easier. I feel like I can manage, even if it's just pretending. I put on my best smile, laugh at jokes, and try to be the person everyone expects me to be. But on the bad days, it feels like a heavy blanket of sadness is draped over me, suffocating and isolating. I don't want to get out of bed, I don't want to talk to anyone, and I don't want to pretend that I'm okay. On those days, I'm quieter, withdrawn, hoping no one notices. I don't want to be asked if I'm okay because the answer is always "no," but I don't want to have to explain why. Sometimes, I don't even know why myself.

In those moments of darkness, my mind becomes my worst enemy. It tells me that I'm not good enough, that I'm a burden, that the world would be better off without me. I started to believe that if I were gone, maybe people would finally see my worth, maybe they would regret the lies they spread, the rumors they believed. But then, in the midst of these thoughts, I think of my mom.

My mother, who has been through so much herself, is the one person who keeps me anchored to this world. I've sacrificed so much of my youth for her, trying to be the daughter she needed, trying to make her proud. I know that if I were to end my life, it would destroy her. She wouldn't survive losing me, and I can't bear the thought of causing her that pain. So, I push through, day after day, fighting this battle in silence, for her.

Depression is a complicated, painful journey that I wouldn't wish on anyone. It's a constant struggle to find light in the darkness, to keep going when every part of me wants to give up. But I keep going, not just for myself, but for my mom, and for the hope that one day, things might get better.

Driving up Topanga Pacific Coast Highway was more than just a routine for me; it was a ritual of peace, a way to escape from the chaos of my life. The winding road, the breathtaking view of the valley from the mountain, and the soothing sound of the ocean in the distance, it all felt like a sanctuary. I'd find myself on that road almost every day, sometimes three times a week, just to clear my head. Even if I didn't stop in Malibu, just the drive itself brought me a sense of calm that I couldn't find anywhere else.

However, as much as that road represented peace, it also became a place where I contemplated ending everything. The dangerous curves, the steep cliffs, and that one particular turn where you can see the entire valley stretched out below you, it was there that I tried to drive off the cliff

four times. Each time, I would speed up as I approached the curve, telling myself that this was the perfect way to go. It would look like an accident, and no one would suspect that it was intentional. They'd just think I lost control, that it was a tragic mistake.

But every time, just as I was about to go through with it, something would stop me. I'd slam on the brakes at the very last second, my heart pounding, my body shaking. I don't know what it was, a guardian angel, a fleeting thought of my mom, or maybe just a deep-seated will to live, but something always held me back. After the fourth time, I realized I couldn't keep testing fate like that. I couldn't keep putting myself in a position where I might actually go through with it.

With that in mind, I stopped driving up PCH. I stopped going to Malibu altogether. The road that once brought me so much peace now triggered overwhelming anxiety. Just thinking about it gave me flashbacks, made me relive those moments where I came so close to ending it all. The place that had once been my escape was now a reminder of how close I came to giving up. I couldn't

face that road anymore, not with the memories it held. Consequently, I had to let it go, finding other ways to cope, other roads to take. But I'll never forget those drives or how something inside me, despite everything, refused to let me go over the edge.

About a year had passed since the last time I had traveled on Topanga PCH, and I had avoided that road like the plague. The memories were too raw, too painful. But one day, my friends suggested we go to the beach to watch the sunset, and I agreed, not thinking much about the route we'd take. We all piled into the car, chatting and laughing, and I was lost in the moment until I looked out the window and realized where we were.

As soon as I saw that familiar stretch of road, my heart dropped. My chest tightened, and I could feel the panic rising inside me. I tried to keep it together, but the tears started flowing uncontrollably. My friends were confused—they had no idea what was going on, and I couldn't bring myself to explain. How could I tell them that I had tried to kill myself on this road, that I had come so close to driving off that cliff? The words were stuck in my throat, and all I could do was sit there silently, tears streaming down my face, while they tried to comfort me without understanding why.

No one asked questions. They could sense it was something deep, something painful, and we all just pretended like nothing happened. But that day was a turning point for me. I realized that I

couldn't keep letting this trauma control me. I had to face it, head-on, no matter how terrifying it was. I promised myself that I would heal, that I would not let those dark memories dictate my life any longer.

A few days later, I got into my car, determined to conquer the fear that had taken hold of me. I drove up PCH by myself, my heart pounding, my hands shaking on the steering wheel. As I approached that turn, the one where I had tried to end it all, I started screaming and crying, the memories flooding back in waves. I relived every moment of those drives, the despair, the hopelessness, the desperation to escape the pain. But through the tears, I kept telling myself, "I'm okay. I'm strong. I can do this."

It wasn't easy. It took me about 7 to 10 more drives up that road before I could do it without breaking down. Each time, it got a little easier, but the sadness was still there, lingering like a shadow. However, with each drive, I felt a bit stronger, a bit more in control. Now, when I take that road, I still feel a twinge of sadness, but I also feel an immense sense of pride. I didn't let that trauma consume me. I faced it, I dealt with it, and I overcame it. That road, which once symbolized my darkest moments, now represents my resilience.

That wasn't the only time I struggled with the urge to end it all. I remember another dark period during high school when things with my parents were particularly rough. We weren't getting along at all, and I felt completely isolated and alone. The weight of it all became too much, and I just wanted to escape, to sleep and never wake up. One night, in a moment of sheer desperation, I swallowed 12 pills of Tylenol PM, hoping it would be a peaceful, painless way to end my life.

I remember feeling drowsy, my eyelids growing heavy as I slipped into unconsciousness. I could hear my mom calling my name, but I couldn't respond, couldn't open my eyes no matter how hard I tried. I thought this was it, that I was dying and this was the end. But then, I felt something cold and wet splashing me. My mom was throwing cold water on me, trying to wake me up. I opened my eyes, disoriented and angry. She was yelling at me, asking why I was sleeping so much, completely unaware of what I had tried to do.

I didn't tell her what I had done. How could I? She just thought I was being lazy or rebellious, and I let her think that. But inside, I was furious. Why couldn't I just die? Why did God keep me alive when I was so miserable, so full of pain and hate for the life I was living? I cried out to God, begging for Him to let me go, to end my suffering.

But God didn't take me, and as much as I resented that at the time, looking back now, I'm grateful. Those moments of despair didn't break me. They were the fire that forged me into the person I am today, stronger, more resilient, and determined to live a life worth living.

It took me years of grappling with the weight of my experiences to finally come to terms with the fact that this is my life and my story. The harsh realities that I've faced are mine to bear, but they are also mine to overcome. I realized that no matter how deep the pain, no matter how overwhelming the darkness, nothing is worth ending my life over. There were countless nights when I would lie in bed, wrestling with the demons inside my head, telling myself over and over again that I wouldn't hurt myself. But I'd be lying if I said I never broke those promises. There were times when the sadness was too much to bear, and I found myself slipping back into old habits, questioning if life was worth all the pain. But somehow, I always managed to find the strength to pull myself out of that darkness.

One thing I've learned is that the simple joys in life can be the most healing. I try to go out and immerse myself in places that bring me peace. Whether it's sitting by the ocean, letting the sound of the waves calm my soul, or hiking up a quiet mountain trail where I can breathe deeply and let go of the weight I carry, these moments of connection with nature ground me. They remind me that life, despite its trials, is inherently beautiful.

I also make an effort to surround myself with people who uplift me, who see the good in me even when I struggle to see it in myself. It's taken time to find those people, but having them in my life has been a blessing. Their support and love have helped me through some of my darkest days. But beyond relying on others, I've learned the importance of self-care. I push myself to get out of bed every day, even when I'd rather stay hidden under the covers. I make a conscious choice to do things that bring me joy, no matter how small they may seem.

Going for walks, especially in the early morning when the world is still waking up, fills me with a sense of calm and purpose. There's something about the fresh air, the stillness, and the quiet beauty of nature that soothes my mind. It's my time to reflect, to breathe, and to remind myself that I am still here, still fighting.

Music and dancing, too, have become my lifeline. There's a freedom in losing myself to the rhythm, in letting my body move in ways that express emotions I can't put into words. When I dance, I feel alive, connected to something greater than myself. It's in those moments, with the music blaring and my feet moving across the floor, that I truly feel happy. It's as if, for those few minutes, all my worries disappear, and I'm just a girl who loves to dance.

These small acts of self-love and care have helped me reclaim my life. They've shown me that, no matter how hard things get, there is always something worth living for. It might be a sunrise, a walk on the beach, a dance under the stars, or the laughter of a friend. These are the moments that make life beautiful. And these are the moments that remind me why I choose to stay.

Chapter: 34
Solitude During COVID

When COVID hit, it was a tough time for everyone around the world. Everyone was on lockdown: no one was able to go anywhere or do anything. I kid you not, I was scared, not because of what was happening with the virus, but because I thought I was going to relapse. I had finally started getting happy in life and being social. When the lockdown occurred, I told myself there was no way I could stay home. I would go crazy; I had never been alone and didn't know how.

I woke up every day and got dressed as if I was going to work. Even though there was nowhere to go, I needed that routine. I would just drive around, and going to Target became my daily escape. I would walk around the store with a mask on, of course, just to feel like I was out in the world, doing something, anything. The act of being out and about, even in such a limited way, helped me maintain my sanity.

But it wasn't just Target that helped me maintain a sense of balance. I would sit at the beach or even at the park for hours, just working remotely from there. The change of scenery was essential. I needed to be outside, to feel the wind on my face, to hear the sounds of life around me. It was in those moments, surrounded by nature, that I found a strange sense of peace and clarity. For me, COVID was truly a blessing in disguise. It forced me to confront my fears of being alone and showed me that I was stronger than I thought. The lockdown became a time of growth. I learned to find joy in the small things, to create my own sense of normalcy amidst the chaos. And in doing so, I discovered a resilience within myself that I never knew existed.

When the restrictions were finally lifted in LA County, and people could slowly start going out again, I made a promise to myself: I was going to take full advantage of this newfound freedom. I didn't care that it was strange or uncomfortable; I was determined to reclaim my sense of normalcy and joy. So, I began taking myself out every single day. Whether it was to a restaurant, a bar, or just to walk around a park, I was out there rediscovering the world and, more importantly, myself.

The idea of going out alone was daunting at first. I had never really spent much time by myself, and the thought of dining or sitting at a bar without anyone by my side felt almost intimidating.

But I pushed through that discomfort, telling myself that this was necessary. I needed to learn how to enjoy my own company, to be okay with just being me, without the need for anyone else to validate my experiences.

One day, I decided to go to the Glendale Galleria, an outdoor mall that's a blend of high-end stores and cozy restaurants. The sun was shining, and it felt like the perfect day to treat myself to a nice lunch. I chose a restaurant with outdoor seating so I could enjoy the weather, and I sat down at a small table by myself.

For the first few minutes, the waiter seemed to overlook me. I watched as he moved around the tables, greeting and serving everyone else. At first, it didn't bother me, I was used to blending into the background. But after a while, it started to feel intentional, like I was invisible. I decided I wasn't going to let that slide. So, I called him over and asked if I could get a drink.

When he finally brought me my cocktail, I could tell he was curious. He kept glancing at me as I sipped my drink, probably wondering why I was alone. After I ordered my second cocktail, he couldn't help but ask, "Are you waiting for someone else to join you?" I laughed and told him no, I was enjoying a solo lunch. He looked surprised, almost shocked. He admitted that he had never seen a woman dining alone like this before.

That's when I realized how rare it is for people to embrace solitude in public spaces. I told him that I actually loved my own company, that there was something liberating about not needing anyone else to have a good time. We ended up talking for a while, and by the end of the meal, I felt like I had made a new friend. He kept checking in on me, bringing me different dishes to try, and we even joked about how I was single-handedly going to eat through the entire menu.

I stayed at that restaurant for hours, savoring every bite and every sip, not just of the food and drinks but of the experience itself. I discovered that day that there's a unique kind of empowerment that comes from being comfortable with yourself, from knowing that you don't need anyone else to feel complete.

Looking back, that day was a turning point for me. It wasn't just about surviving the lockdown or dealing with the aftermath of the pandemic—it was about thriving in my own space, about finding joy and peace in who I am, even when I'm alone. That sense of independence, of being able to sit alone at a table and be perfectly content, is something I carry with me every day now. It's a reminder that I am enough, just as I am.

Since that day, I started indulging in activities I had always enjoyed but never really took the time to do alone. I began going to the movies by myself, something I had never done before. I'd bring a small blanket and sneak in some snacks—my little act of rebellion. Sitting in the dark theater, I'd see couples cuddling, and while there were moments of loneliness, I reminded myself that watching a movie in a theater was just like watching one at home alone—only with better sound and a bigger screen. It became a peaceful ritual for me, a time to escape into different worlds without needing anyone else to accompany me.

I also discovered a love for spending hours at hookah lounges. I'd take a book with me, find a cozy corner, and just read for as long as I wanted. Those afternoons were some of my favorite times because I felt so in tune with who I was becoming. I found myself truly enjoying my own company, savoring the solitude and the sense of independence that came with it. Nothing and no one could disturb my peace in those moments.

However, when the world began to open up again after COVID, I faced a new challenge: how to be social again. During the lockdown, I had cut myself off from everyone, relishing the solitude and the personal growth it brought. But now, with restrictions lifted and people eager to reconnect, I found myself resistant to the idea of rejoining the social scene. My friends would call me every day, inviting me to go out and catch up, but I kept declining. I had become so accustomed to my own space and time that the thought of being around others felt overwhelming. It reached a point where I stopped going out altogether. I stayed home most of the time, enjoying the quiet and the comfort of being by myself. My mom would notice and encourage me to socialize more, but I just didn't want to. I had found so much peace in my own company that the idea of mingling with others felt like an intrusion.

After a month or two of this, I began to realize that my isolation was becoming unhealthy. While I enjoyed being alone, I also recognized the importance of maintaining connections with others. So, I slowly started to reintegrate into the social world. I began going out once or twice a week, catching up with friends I hadn't seen in a long time. Yet, even then, I would find myself getting bored after just 45 minutes of conversation. My mind would wander, and I'd start longing for the solitude I had grown to love.

To balance this, I made a pact with myself: one day out of the week would be solely dedicated to me. It became my "self-care day," where I would do whatever I desired, whether it was indulging in a full spa day at home or treating myself to a solo wine and dine experience. These days became my sanctuary, a time to recharge and reconnect with myself amidst the busyness of life. This new approach allowed me to find a balance between my love for solitude and the need to maintain relationships. It reminded me that it's okay to cherish time alone while also staying connected with the people who matter. In the end, I learned that it's all about finding harmony between being social and nurturing the relationship I have with myself.

Chapter: 35
Understanding Faith

Growing up, my understanding of Islam was quite limited. My parents didn't focus much on teaching me the religious practices or deeper meanings behind our faith. I knew the basics—like the significance of Ramadan, Eid, and a few other holidays—but that was pretty much it. As I got older, especially in my teenage years, my mom's side of the family began to pressure me more about learning and practicing Islam. They'd often talk about how important it was to pray, read the Quran, and follow Islamic principles. But I'm someone who doesn't respond well to being forced into anything. The more they pushed, the more I found myself resisting.

Around the age of 25 or 26, something inside me shifted. I realized that I wanted to know more about Islam, but not because anyone was telling me to. It was a personal desire to understand my faith on my own terms. One of the main reasons was the thought of my future children. I always imagined raising them with a solid foundation in Islam, sending them to Islamic school, and making sure they knew the things I didn't learn growing up. But how could I expect them to embrace something that I hadn't fully embraced myself? That thought was a turning point for me.

I decided to take matters into my own hands. I started small, learning how to pray. At first, it was just once or twice a day, but I gradually worked up to praying three times daily. It wasn't perfect, but it was a start. I used YouTube as my guide, following along with prayer tutorials and learning the Arabic words and movements step by step. It was a slow process, but every small accomplishment felt like a victory.

Learning to pray in Arabic was particularly challenging, but also incredibly rewarding. I remember the first time I completed a full prayer in Arabic... it felt like such a huge achievement.

I was proud of myself for taking the initiative, for doing it on my own terms, and for not letting the pressures and opinions of others dictate my relationship with my faith.

This journey wasn't just about learning to pray; it was about discovering a part of myself that I had never really connected with before. It was empowering to realize that I could make this faith my own, that I could learn and grow in it at my own pace. It also made me more confident in the idea of raising my future children with these values because I was living them myself.

Even though I'm not perfect in my practice, and I still have a lot to learn, the fact that I started this journey is something I'll always be proud of. It's a reminder that sometimes the most important steps we take are the ones we take on our own, not because someone else is telling us to, but because we feel it's the right thing for us.

As I began to embrace my faith more, my parents started to grow concerned. They noticed the changes in my routine and the newfound dedication I had toward Islam, and it worried them. My dad, in particular, was puzzled by what he saw as a sudden shift. He sat me down multiple times, asking why I was so deeply invested in practicing Islam all of a sudden. He seemed to think that perhaps there was an external influence, a man, perhaps, pushing me in this direction. I had to reassure him that this journey was purely for myself, driven by a genuine desire to understand and connect with my faith, not because of anyone else.

Don't get me wrong, I love my religion. I find comfort and strength in the practices and the connection it gives me to something greater. But I also have my reservations. There are aspects of Islam that I struggle with, things that don't align with my personal beliefs or the way I want to live my life. It's a complicated relationship, one that I navigate carefully. I don't want to get into all the details because I respect that everyone has their own beliefs, and I don't want to disrespect those who are devout. But for me, my practice of Islam is more about the personal connection with God than following every rule to the letter.

For years, I've found myself connecting with God in my own way. Instead of adhering strictly to the five daily prayers, I often just sit and talk to God. It's usually at night when I'm alone in the car driving home that I feel the strongest urge to reach out. I'll look up at the sky, at the stars or the moon, and just talk, sometimes out loud, sometimes in my head. I tell God about my day, my worries, my hopes, and fears. It's a simple, personal ritual that brings me a lot of peace.

And then there are the moments that feel like miracles. I know it sounds crazy, and maybe it's hard to believe, but there have been times when I've been so overwhelmed, so stressed, that I just cry out to God, asking for a sign, for some kind of help. And within minutes, I'll receive exactly what I needed. It's like my prayers are answered almost instantly, in ways that I can't explain.

It's these moments that strengthen my faith, that make me believe that even though I don't follow every rule perfectly, God is still there, listening to me, understanding me, and showing me that I'm not alone. It's this personal relationship with God, one that isn't bound by strict rules or rituals, is what keeps me grounded. It's not about how often I pray or how much scripture I've memorized; it's about the conversations I have with God, the trust I put in Him, and the way I see His presence in my life, especially in those small, miraculous moments that remind me that everything is going to be Okay.

I celebrate Muslim holidays, but I also celebrate Christmas with some of my family. Yes, I am Muslim by birth, but I always felt like I needed to learn more about other religions to see where my heart truly lies. It's not that I'm considering converting—I just feel so lost, like I've drifted far from God and need to find a way back. But I don't want to go to the extreme of being overly religious; I'm searching for balance, a way to integrate faith into my life that feels authentic and grounded.

One day, in the most unexpected of circumstances, I met this random man who was an Orthodox Christian. We were both at this quiet café and somehow, we ended up in a deep conversation about life. There was something incredibly calming about talking to him— like he was exactly who I needed to meet at that moment. We talked about our beliefs, our doubts, and our struggles. He shared that he also sought a balanced approach to his faith, not wanting to be confined by rigid doctrines but still wanting to maintain a connection to God. It was like we were on the same wavelength, understanding each other in a way that was rare.

I confessed to him how lost I've been feeling lately, not just in life but especially with my religion. I explained how I've been struggling to reconnect with God and how distant I've felt from everything I once believed in. I told him that I wanted to find my way back but wasn't sure how to do it, that I was looking for a path that would help me rediscover myself and my faith without feeling forced or unnatural.

He listened carefully and then offered a suggestion that really resonated with me. He told me that maybe I should visit his church just once to speak with their priest. He emphasized that going to church or speaking to a priest didn't mean I was converting or making any drastic changes.

Instead, he said it could be a way to explore another path, to gain some guidance, and perhaps find the direction I was looking for. His words were so reassuring; it felt like a light bulb went off in my head.

I loved the idea, especially because I knew that if I went to a mosque and spoke to a Sheik, I might be met with judgment or pressure that I wasn't ready to face. I needed a space where I could speak openly about everything I was going through without the fear of being criticized or looked down upon. I wanted to be able to express my doubts, my fears, and my hopes without holding back.

The thought of taking that first step, of actually going to this church, both excited and terrified me. It was a step into the unknown, and I knew it could potentially change the way I saw everything. But I also knew that it was something I had to do for myself, something that could bring me the clarity and peace I was desperately seeking.

At the same time, I was scared, scared that my best friend or my family would find out and start questioning me. I didn't want to have to defend my choices or explain myself to anyone. I didn't want them to try to change my mind or steer me back onto a path they thought was right for me. This was my journey, my personal quest for understanding and connection, and I needed to navigate it on my own terms.

In the end, I realized that this is my life, and I'm the only one who can figure out what's right for me. No one else can walk this path for me, and no one else can tell me what's in my heart. This journey is mine to take, and while it's daunting, it's also incredibly empowering to know that I'm in control of where I go from here.

When I was going through my religious phase, I was deeply committed to finding a spiritual path that resonated with me. I took it very seriously, to the point where I would literally pull over my car in the middle of a drive just to pray if the time came. It didn't matter where I was or what I was doing; when it was time to pray, I would make sure to stop everything and focus on my connection with God. It was a time in my life where I felt that this was the way to truly be devout. I started covering up more, ensuring that not an inch of skin was visible. I even began to contemplate wearing a hijab, something that no one in my family had ever done. The thought of taking that step felt monumental because I knew how shocked my family would be. I hesitated for a long time, wondering how they would react and whether I was truly ready for the commitment that the hijab symbolized.

During this phase, I met a guy named Zack. It was during the COVID lockdown, and with the world at a standstill, there wasn't much to do but talk and get to know each other. Zack was a Pakistani man, very polite and seemingly grounded. We started hanging out a lot, and at first, it was nice to have someone to talk to, especially since he was also going through his own religious journey. It felt like we were on similar paths, trying to get closer to God and make sense of the world in the midst of chaos.

But as time went on, I began to notice that Zack's path was taking a much more extreme turn. His journey toward God became less about spirituality and more about strict dogma. He started to become extremely religious in a way that bordered on fanaticism. Zack began making videos where he would rant about how society was corrupt, how everyone who didn't follow his strict interpretation of Islam was doomed, and that we should all be punished for straying from the "true" path. It was alarming to watch him go from being a nice, understanding guy to someone who couldn't see the world in anything but black and white.

I tried to reason with him, telling him that everyone is entitled to their own beliefs and that he should focus on his own journey rather than trying to impose his views on others. But Zack didn't see it that way. He became increasingly controlling, especially with me. He started dictating what I could and couldn't wear, insisting that skinny jeans and shirts that showed my shoulders were inappropriate and sinful. It got to the point where I felt like I was losing myself, but for some reason, I started to listen to him. I think part of me wanted to be supportive, to be a "good Muslim," even if I didn't agree with half the things he was saying or doing. I purged my wardrobe of anything remotely fashionable or revealing and replaced it with the most modest, conservative clothes I could find.

It wasn't just about dressing modestly; it was about conforming to Zack's increasingly rigid and oppressive standards.

Zack's controlling behavior didn't stop at my wardrobe. He began to take control over more aspects of my life, deciding where I could go, who I could talk to, and even how I should think.

He was relentless in his criticism, not just of me but of everyone around me, especially my family. He would talk so negatively about them, calling them sinners and saying they were leading me astray. It hurt deeply because, despite everything, I loved my family and didn't appreciate someone I barely knew passing such harsh judgments. I would get into huge fights with him, defending my family and telling him that he had no right to disrespect them. I told him that just because I wasn't bad-mouthing his dysfunctional, low-life family didn't give him the right to attack mine. But Zack never backed down, and the tension between us kept growing.

The breaking point came one day when I got extremely sick. I was with Zack when I suddenly passed out. Instead of calling 911 or trying to help me, Zack did something that left me utterly disgusted—he started taking pictures of me while I was unconscious. When I later confronted him about why he didn't help, he told me that if anything happened to me, he wanted to have proof that he wasn't involved. He said it so casually like it was the most logical thing in the world, but it made my stomach turn. I realized then that I was in a dangerous situation, not just physically but emotionally and mentally. This was a man who was supposed to care about me, yet he was more concerned with protecting himself than making sure I was okay.

That was the moment I knew I had to get out. Zack had become a toxic influence in my life, pushing me further away from the person I wanted to be. I realized that I didn't want to live in fear or under someone else's control. I wanted to have my own relationship with God, one that was built on love, understanding, and personal growth, not fear, judgment, and oppression. So, I started to pull away from Zack, slowly at first and then more decisively. I began reclaiming my life, my beliefs, and my identity. It wasn't easy, but I knew it was the only way to truly be at peace with myself and my faith.

Zack wanted to marry me, and when he brought up the idea, I felt a mix of emotions—fear, desperation, and a faint hope that maybe this could be a way out. I told my family about him, and as I expected, my parents were hesitant. They didn't feel like Zack was a good match for me; they saw the red flags even before I did. They knew I deserved someone who would truly cherish and respect me, not control and belittle me. But at that time, I was so desperate to escape my home situation and find some semblance of independence that I convinced myself marrying Zack might be a good idea. I wanted to believe that maybe, just maybe, marriage would make things better. Even though I knew deep down that Zack was not the right person for me, I chose to ignore those instincts. I thought that getting married would somehow solve my problems, that it would bring me happiness and stability.

Zack, however, had a very different idea of what our future together would look like. He didn't want to have a wedding at all, which was odd considering how much importance our culture places on such celebrations. He lost his job during the pandemic and had no income coming in. When I asked him how he planned to support us, especially since he had no job prospects on the horizon, his answer shocked me. He told me that my income was more than enough for both of us. He was completely comfortable with the idea of living off my earnings without contributing anything financially himself. He didn't even seem to feel any shame about it.

That was the moment a switch flipped in my mind. I kid you not, when I heard those words come out of his mouth, I felt a rush of clarity. This wasn't just a bad idea; it was a potential disaster. I realized that Zack wasn't just looking for a partner, he was looking for a way to coast through life without putting in any effort. He was getting used to me taking care of everything, from buying groceries to cooking, cleaning, and basically managing the household. I was doing everything a wife is expected to do and more, without any of the love, support, or partnership that should come with it. And yet, it was never good enough for him. No matter how much I did, Zack always found something to criticize, something to demand more of.

Chapter: 36
When It Rains, It Pours

I started to see that I was on the brink of leaving one miserable, unhappy life only to step into another one that could be even worse. I thought about what it would mean to marry Zack, to be tied to him legally, financially, and emotionally for the rest of my life. The thought terrified me. I imagined what it would be like to bring a child into that situation, to raise a child in a household where their father was more interested in controlling me than in being a loving, supportive partner and parent. I saw my entire future play out in my mind, and it wasn't a future I wanted. It was a future filled with resentment, regret, and a deep, unending unhappiness.

I knew I couldn't do it. I couldn't marry Zack. I couldn't sentence myself to a life of misery just because I was too afraid to admit that I had made a mistake. So, I made the hardest decision I've ever had to make—I called off the whole thing. I told Zack I couldn't marry him, that I didn't want to spend my life being unhappy and unfulfilled. He was furious, of course. He didn't take it well at all, but I didn't care. I had to put myself first for once, and I had to do what was right for me, even if it meant breaking someone else's heart. I had to choose my own happiness, my own peace of mind, over a life of constant struggle and dissatisfaction.

Walking away from Zack wasn't easy, but it was necessary. I knew that if I had gone through with the marriage, I would have regretted it for the rest of my life. I had to trust myself, trust that I deserved better, and trust that I would find happiness on my own terms. And so, I left Zack behind and started a new chapter in my life, one where I was finally free to pursue my own dreams and live the life I wanted, not the life someone else wanted for me. What is my life like lately?

Do I hear you ask me what I have been doing lately and what my life has been like? Fast forward to June 2023, I was working at a fertility clinic in Brentwood, and I had been there for about eight months. I genuinely loved my job because it involved helping women get pregnant and supporting them through their fertility journey. It felt fulfilling to be part of such a significant chapter in these women's lives. But on June 16th, I was having a particularly rough day. I was feeling really sick, constantly dizzy, and I knew something wasn't right. I kept telling my manager that I needed to go home, but she insisted I try to push through the day and only leave if my symptoms got worse.

By 1 pm, I knew I couldn't stay any longer. I tried calling my manager to let her know I had to leave, but she wasn't picking up her phone. Feeling desperate, I decided to walk across the street to find her and let her know in person that I was leaving. The elevators in the building weren't working, so I took the stairs. As I was walking down, the dizziness intensified. I let go of the railing to hold my head, hoping to stop the spinning, but that decision turned out to be a mistake.

My foot slipped, and before I knew it, I was tumbling down a flight of steps. I bashed my head against the wall and landed hard on my neck and back at the bottom of the stairwell.

Everything after that is a blur. I don't remember much except waking up to the sound of my colleague calling my name and the sight of paramedics surrounding me. I was in tears from the unbearable pain that was radiating through my body. I was rushed to the hospital, and all I could think of was my parents. I was terrified, crying out for them, feeling more vulnerable than I had in years. My colleague, who had followed me to the hospital, was kind enough to call my parents from Santa Monica Hospital to let them know what had happened. It was one of the scariest moments of my life, and all I could do was pray that I would be okay.

As my parents rushed to the hospital, I was overwhelmed with anxiety, feeling the familiar grip of PTSD tightening around me. The memories of the last time I was in a hospital as a child came flooding back, making everything more terrifying. I couldn't shake the feeling of being trapped, wanting desperately to go home but unable to move. My body was in agony; it felt as though I had been hit by a bus. My face was covered in bruises, and every inch of me ached.

When my parents finally arrived, I felt a wave of relief, but it was quickly overshadowed by fear as the doctors rushed me off for a CT scan to check for any injuries to my head. The hours that followed felt like an eternity. I lay there, waiting, each second dragging by as I wondered what the scan would reveal. When the doctor finally came back with the results, he told me I had a severe concussion and needed to rest as much as possible to allow my body to heal. The news was both a relief and a new source of anxiety. After over nine hours in the hospital, I finally was allowed to go home, and I left, bruised, sore, and exhausted. However, the fear of what might come next haunted me all the way home.

The weekend passed in a blur of pain and worry, but I knew I had to go back to work on Monday, just two days after the accident. I knew I wasn't ready. I tried to push through, and I kept telling my manager that I wasn't okay. Staring at the computer screen made me feel sicker by the minute, the dizziness and nausea never really subsided. For a month, I dragged myself to work, sitting in the dark because any kind of light was unbearable. The constant dizziness was making it impossible to function.

After multiple visits to different doctors, I finally saw a neurologist who confirmed what I already knew deep down—I wasn't okay. He told me that I needed to be on complete disability until further notice that my body needed time to heal from the trauma it had endured. I was devastated. I hadn't worked for a year now, and the aftermath of my fall had left me in a state I barely recognized. My brain had suffered from inflammation and swelling, causing a host of other issues, including sensory nerve damage and impaired hearing. The most basic things, like hearing properly, had become a struggle. My world felt muffled, distant, and I found myself withdrawing more and more from people because I couldn't bear the embarrassment of not being able to hear them or having to ask them to repeat themselves.

The worst part was the stuttering. I had never had trouble speaking before, but now, I found myself struggling to get my words out, feeling self-conscious and vulnerable in ways I never had before. I was embarrassed, convinced that people were judging me, not understanding the extent of what I was going through. On top of everything, I was dealing with memory loss. Simple things would slip my mind, and I would berate myself, feeling like I should be better and stronger.

As time went on, I had to learn to be kinder to myself, to accept that healing is a journey, not a destination. My accident wasn't a small thing; it was a significant trauma that my body and mind are still recovering from. I reminded myself daily that I needed to be patient, that with time, things would improve, and I would regain my health. The journey has definitely been long and lonely, filled with moments of doubt and despair. Still, I hold onto hope, knowing that I will come out of this stronger, more resilient, and more compassionate toward myself.

I no longer look for happiness in other people, but I do seek that sense of comfort—someone who will stand by me through both the good and bad times. My life seems to have more lows than highs, but I am determined to change that, to tip the scales in favor of the highs. I realize that I don't give myself enough credit for the positive things that have been happening to me. I have let the negativity overshadow everything, allowing it to take a toll on me. I want to break free from this pattern by letting the wins, no matter how small, lead me to happiness instead of allowing the lows to consume my life.

Here is an example. One day, I was driving down Ventura Blvd during rush hour, chatting with a friend on my way to the mall. The day had been hot, and I was already feeling the discomfort of a sunburn from a beach trip earlier. Out of nowhere, my steering wheel was completely locked. I couldn't turn left or right, and panic set in. My car would only go straight, and then the battery light flickered on while the air conditioning suddenly cut out. I had no idea what was happening, but I knew it wasn't good. Somehow, I managed to pull over and turn on my emergency lights. My heart was racing as I called AAA, thinking maybe the car battery had died and just needed a jump.

When the tow truck finally arrived, the driver checked my car and told me that the battery was fine, but the alternator had died, and the steering wheel belt had broken. The stress hit me like a wave. I didn't know what to do next. I called one of my older cousins, sobbing on the phone, overwhelmed by the situation. There's something uniquely frustrating about car problems, they can make you feel completely helpless. I was already debating whether I should get a new car, but with my bad credit and lack of funds, even fixing my current car seemed impossible.

I ended up towing my car to my cousin's house and just sat at the kitchen table, staring at nothing, trying to figure out what my options were. Hours passed, and my cousin kept asking why I was so upset. He didn't understand why I was so stressed out. He kept telling me to look on the bright side, that at least I had an excuse to get a new car, and I should be thankful that I didn't get into an accident or face something more serious. But all I could think about was money, how much it was going to cost to fix the car, how I was going to explain this to my dad, and the dread of going home to face the situation.

Eventually, I arranged for another tow truck to take my car from my cousin's house to my home. My mom was waiting for me outside when I arrived, and instead of the anger or disappointment I was expecting, she was just relieved that I was okay. Her concern for my safety over everything else brought a sense of calm that I desperately needed at that moment. But even as I tried to find comfort in her relief, I couldn't shake the weight of everything else pressing down on me, the financial strain, the fear of what my dad would say, and the uncertainty of what would happen next.

It's been three weeks since my car broke down, and let me tell you, the struggle is real. Relying on Uber for everything, from getting to my appointments to running basic errands, has been draining my wallet faster than I can keep up. The costs are adding up, and it feels like I'm bleeding money just to keep up with the basics. Amid all this, my dad mentioned he saw a Tesla he really liked at the mall and wanted me to check it out. At first, I was excited; the idea of driving a Tesla was thrilling, but then reality hit me. Could I really afford a new car right now? The thought of taking on such a big financial commitment was terrifying.

That day, we went to see the car. The Tesla was sleek and beautiful, everything I could want in a car, but I couldn't shake the anxiety gnawing at me. My dad, however, was all in. He kept pushing me, practically shoving me toward the decision to buy the car right then and there. But he didn't understand that I needed time to think this through, to figure out if it was a financially sound decision for me. When I tried to explain this, he lashed out right there in the dealership, in front of everyone.

I could feel the tears welling up, but I forced them back, not wanting to break down in front of him or the salespeople. It felt like I was being pressured into something I wasn't ready for, and the worst part was that my dad wasn't offering any real help, no advice, no support, just demands. At that moment, I stood up for myself, even though my voice was shaking with the effort to hold back my emotions. "NO. I will not buy the car today. I need time to think," I told him, even as tears streamed down my face. It was one of the hardest things I've had to do, standing up to him like that.

When I got home, I didn't have the energy for anything else. I went straight to my room, crawled into bed, and didn't get out for the rest of the day. The anger and depression weighed on me like a heavy blanket. All I wanted was for my dad to approach the situation differently, to say, "Let me help you. Let's find a smart way to do this." But instead, he just tried to force his will on me, not understanding—or maybe not caring, about what I was going through. It's like he always thinks he's right about everything, even when he's clearly not.

As much as I resented his approach, he's still my dad. I have to accept him for who he is, both the good and the bad. That's a hard pill to swallow, especially when you're trying to navigate life's challenges on your own, and the person who's supposed to guide you only makes it harder. It's exhausting, but it's the reality I'm learning to live with.

The next day, I decided to move forward with the car application to see if I would even get accepted. My heart was pounding as I submitted the form, hoping against hope that, somehow, I might get a break. But, as I feared, the answer was no—I was rejected because of my poor credit. The disappointment was overwhelming, but I wasn't ready to give up. I had one last option: having my mom cosign for me. Thankfully, she agreed without hesitation, and I felt a weight lift off my shoulders. If it wasn't for my mom stepping in, I would have been completely screwed.

I'm still in the process of figuring out if getting a new car is the best option for me, but at least now I have some hope. I'm grateful that my friends have also been incredibly supportive, offering to either pay to get my car fixed or help with the down payment. Their generosity means the world to me, and it's one of the few things keeping me afloat during this tough time. Between my mom and my friends, this experience provided a win with enough happiness to help balance the lows of the whole situation.

June was probably one of the shittiest months of my life. My health took a nosedive, and I was constantly sick every single day. I felt like my body was betraying me. It got so bad that I felt like I needed to be hospitalized. I was miserable because I knew something wasn't right, but no one could figure out what was going on. For three weeks, I was stuck in bed, more often than not, dealing with a sore throat, fever, or severe toothache. To top it all off, I got the worst sunburn of my life. I'm not someone who burns easily; if anything, I stay pale as a ghost. But this time, the sun had other plans. I couldn't sleep for three days straight because the burns were so bad. My skin peeled for days, and nothing I did seemed to help.

As if that wasn't enough, I had been using Garnier shampoo for three weeks, and to my horror, half of my long hair, hair that used to fall past my chest—broke off. I was devastated. My once beautiful, long hair was now chopped off at chin level, and I cried more than I ever have over anything in my life. I had heard horror stories about people losing their hair, but never in a million years did I think it would happen to me.

I don't know why all of this is happening. It feels like the universe is conspiring against me, but I'm trying so hard not to let the negativity consume me. I've had multiple meltdowns, but somewhere deep down, I'm telling myself that maybe this is all happening for a reason. Maybe something good is coming my way, and this is just the universe's way of clearing out the old to make room for the new. Losing my hair was devastating, but I'm choosing to see it as a fresh start, a way to let go of all the negative, toxic energy that has been weighing me down.

Chapter: 37
I Will Thrive

I know that when you're in the middle of a storm, it's hard to see the light. All you see is the darkness, and trust me, I'm no stranger to that. I'm an overthinker, a worrier, and someone who often lets negativity take over. But I'm also a forgiving person, someone who would go above and beyond for anyone in need. And yes, that has led to me being taken advantage of more times than I can count, but it hasn't stopped me from trying to be a better person every day.

I laugh and smile, no matter what kind of day I'm having, because I know that somewhere out there, someone is going through something worse. Sometimes, though, I wish someone would just give me a shoulder to cry on and tell me everything is going to be okay. The reality is, everyone is going through something. Some people show their pain, while others hide it, but we all have our struggles.

I've worked hard on myself to become the person I am today. I'm a work in progress, and at 29 years old, I still have my whole life ahead of me. I know that bigger and better things are on the horizon. I may not have found my happy ending yet, but I believe that it's out there, waiting for me with the right person who truly wants to be with me. Life is full of obstacles, but that's what makes it beautiful. Not every day is going to be rainbows and butterflies—there will be tough days, too. But those tough days make you stronger, and that's something I have to remind myself every day.

You can't trust everyone around you, but that doesn't mean you have to be secretive about your life. If you feel like you need to vent, then do it—find that safe space where you can express yourself without fear of judgment. Never be ashamed to ask for help, and never feel like you're alone in this world. I made a promise to Henry that I would never hurt myself again, and if I ever had the thought of it, I would speak up. Yes, that is a huge promise to make, and it's a heavy burden to carry, but I know what I mean to the people around me. I understand now that if I were to hurt myself, I would be selfish because I would be hurting all those who care about me.

I hope more women in the Middle Eastern community find the courage to speak up because, trust me, I know I am not the only one who went through abuse growing up. It's okay to be scared. It's okay to feel vulnerable. You're not doing anything wrong by speaking up. Silence only perpetuates the cycle of pain and suffering. I've learned through my own journey that if I want to make a difference in any kind of way, I must change my mindset first. I must make a difference in my own life before I can help others. It's not easy, but it's necessary.

Who knows what the future holds for me, but I know I'm excited about whatever is going to happen. I've faced many challenges, but each one has taught me something valuable. I've been through a lot, but I know that others have been through worse. This is my story, and I hope that by sharing it, I can help someone who feels stuck or hopeless. What doesn't kill you makes you stronger, and that's the truth I cling to, even on the darkest days. For now, I thank you for coming with me on this journey through my life. This isn't the ending of my story; it's just the beginning of a new chapter. And I can't wait to share what's next.

Acknowledgements

I would like to thank a couple of people who have truly helped me get my story out there. We spent more than a year getting everything together, working endlessly to make my vision Come true. I would love by starting with my parents, I am the person I am today because of them. I wouldn't change a thing because I learned a lot from them both, my likes and dislikes.

To my Mom,

I love you more than you can imagine. I know life was never easy or fair to you but you showed me strength and courage. I learned so much from you Mommy. I learned to fight for myself no matter what obstacle I faced in life. I learned not everyone is a friend and trust isn't something I should give out so easily. I know you sacrificed a lot for me and always tried your best to make sure I was always happy. I love the relationship we have now, I just wish it was always like this. Mommy, you're the only reason why I'm breathing today. I live for you every day and if you're not here with me on this earth I don't know what I would do without you. I don't know how to live a life without you, you're my mom and thinking about being alone one day without you scares me tremendously. I have no family of my own yet, I have no one that loves or cares for me the way you do. I need you to keep fighting for me mom, I want you to live a long life so you can one day see me get married and have a family of my own.

To my Dad,

I don't even know how to start this. Good or bad you're still my father. I respect you more than you can imagine. I wish I was the son you always wanted. I wish I was the daughter that you screamed to the world about how proud you were of me. I wish you would have realized earlier in my life that I need a father figure more than anything. I know everything you did was a way of making sure I stayed out of trouble. I don't agree with your parenting skills, but I can say that I learned a lot from you. I'm happy that in the last two years, we've tried to build a better relationship with me, and even though we have never spoken about the past, I want you to know I have forgiven you for everything because you're my dad, and I love you. I know life wasn't easy on either of us, but I can now understand why you were the way you were with me. I turned out to be a pretty amazing woman if you ask me. I hope one day I can have the courage to tell you I wrote this book, and I hope you will finally be proud of me. I hope one day you'll hug and kiss me and just tell me you feel beyond blessed to have a daughter like me who has scarified more than any child would for her parents. I don't regret anything dad, I raised myself and have been the most independent person because of you. I thank you because without your tough love I don't know who I would be today.

To Henry

Thank you, Henry, for coming into my life and shaping me into this amazing woman. You always directed me in the right direction. Your love has given me a new meaning to life. I always think of you no matter what I am doing or what decisions I am making in my life. You play a huge role in my life and I can't thank you enough for everything you have done for me. Yes, our relationship has been rocky, but I truly believe no love has it easy. We both have been tested in many ways but only to come out stronger. Thank you for always being my rock and protector. I love you.

Thank you, Ariana, for taking the time out and always helping me edit my book. Thank you for believing in me and my story. If it wasn't for you, I truly don't believe that I would have been

able to finish this book. I would have given up, but you saw something in me and believed that I had a story to tell. Your dedication and efforts you have put into this book means the world to me. I can never thank you enough.

Milton Keynes UK
Ingram Content Group UK Ltd.
UKHW020021271124
451585UK00013B/1379

9 798330 556816